# Freedom in Covenant

# Freedom in Covenant

Reflections on the Distinctive Values and Practices
of the Christian Church (Disciples of Christ)

## Robert D. Cornwall

Foreword by
Mark G. Toulouse

WIPF & STOCK · Eugene, Oregon

FREEDOM IN COVENANT
Reflections on the Distinctive Values and Practices of the Christian Church
(Disciples of Christ)

Wipf & Stock
An Imprint of Wipf and Stock Publishers
199 W. 8th Ave., Suite 3
Eugene, OR 97401

www.wipfandstock.com

ISBN 13: 978-1-4982-2323-2

Manufactured in the U.S.A.                                    08/18/2015

# Contents

# Preamble to *The Design of the Christian Church (Disciples of Christ)*

As members of the Christian Church,

We confess that Jesus is the Christ, the Son of the Living God, and proclaim him Lord and Savior of the world.

In Christ's name and by his grace we accept our mission of witness and service to all people.

We rejoice in God, maker of heaven and earth, and in the covenant of love that binds us to God and one another.

Through baptism into Christ we enter into newness of life and are made one with the whole people of God.

In the communion of the Holy Spirit we are joined together in discipleship and in obedience to Christ.

At the table of the Lord we celebrate with thanksgiving the saving acts and presence of Christ.

Within the universal church we receive the gift of ministry and the light of Scripture.

In the bonds of Christian faith we yield ourselves to God that we may serve the One whose kingdom has no end.

Blessing, glory, and honor be to God forever. Amen.

# Acknowledgments

THE FOUNDATION FOR THIS book was laid in a series of sermons preached at the three Disciples congregations I have served as pastor: First Christian Church of Santa Barbara, California; First Christian Church of Lompoc, California; and Central Woodward Christian Church of Troy, Michigan. I would like to commend each of these congregations for joining me in wrestling with the question of what it means to be part of the Christian Church (Disciples of Christ). I would like to also thank Steve Kindle, Jerry Gladson, Brian Morse, and Keith Watkins for reading the manuscript and making helpful comments. I am blessed to have Mark Toulouse write the foreword to this book, as my own reflections on Disciples values and practices emerged from my reading of his book *Joined in Discipleship: The Shaping of Contemporary Disciples Identity*. I also wish to thank the staff of Wipf and Stock, including my editor, Matthew Wimer, for bringing this book to the public eye. Finally, I must give thanks for my patient spouse, Cheryl, who has allowed me the freedom to pursue the ministry of writing.

# Foreword

Many who pick up this book may well ask why anyone is interested in doing denominational history. Certainly, we live in a postdenominational century. People hop between and among denominations without thinking anything about it. Many congregations actually hide their denominational affiliation—if they actively maintain one at all anymore. Congregations also largely want to keep their money at home. Denominational institutions are desperately trying to downsize as the flow of money from churches dries up dramatically compared to even just a decade ago. Denominations just don't seem to matter. Catholic schools hire Protestants. Protestant churches often work outside denominational apparatus in hiring their next minister. Large numbers of people are leaving denominations every day to attend various mega- and meta-churches where they can pick and choose based on their assessment of just how they want their various needs met. In mentioning the movement of people out of denominations, those in the church must also admit that significant numbers simply leave, never to return to any church, no matter its name or affiliation. Denominationalism seems nearly dead, barely hanging onto any life at all. Denominations? Why pay any attention to them at all anymore?

One answer might be related to the whole notion of Christian identity. What does it mean to be Christian? How does one learn the meaning of Christianity, or experience the practices related to it, or understand the importance of faith and what it represents?

One can, of course, go it alone. Many have tried, but most of those have been long forgotten in the annals of human history. Surely, it is also true that congregations, completely independent from one another and totally separate from denominational identifications, offer one kind of answer to these kinds of questions. But how do they connect with a larger community, or larger Christian concerns and forms than those found in the parochial or ethnocentric qualities associated with only a local congregation?

Denominations offer at least a viable alternative to gaining access to an understanding of Christian identity that challenges us to become better Christians than we might be at present. For all their shortcomings—and they are legion—denominations possess some kind of history, a history of struggles with culture, engagements and activities meant to make for a better world, failures and disappointments, hopes and successes, and a track record of attempts to understand themselves and what it means to be human in light of lived experience and encounter with God. All of that history—the stuff of human lives and of churches and their interactions across the ages—is informative, and even necessary, when one thinks about what it means to call oneself a Christian.

Denominations also struggle with beliefs through time. In all cases, no matter how much they might try to deny it, they provide an argument against the belief that there is such a thing as an identity that stands still, remains the same, and represents only a singular or literal version of Christianity for all time. Christianity cannot be defined by either the premodern or precritical interpretation of the texts or the practices of the majority in our own day. Christian identity must truly be defined over the long haul of history, and the witness of those who are associated with the testimony and ministry of Jesus. Denominations provide countless case-study examples of how to wrestle with biblical texts and their interpretations, with ethics in the practice of Christianity, with liturgies and worship, and with all the various and complicated elements associated with God's mission in the world. The truth is that denominations matter because they have a history that we can engage. They offer a window to an experience and understanding of both times and people representing something other than our own. In short, we can truly learn something about ourselves and the meaning of Christian identity through examining the identity and practices of "the cloud of witnesses" surrounding us in the realm of human history (in the language of Hebrews 12). Denominations that take their history seriously can help us to do that. They can provide us with an avenue into examining ourselves, and learning, ultimately, what it means to be Christian in our contemporary world.

This book makes the effort to remind Disciples, in very accessible form, of their history. In these pages you will encounter something of the nature of Christian freedom as it relates to human freedom and to the freedom found in the practice of biblical interpretation, especially when done in the midst of community. Here you will meet people who sought some form of authority upon which they could depend, an authority willing to engage questions, without falling prey to ever-present temptations to provide overly simplistic answers. You will learn about the importance of unity within God's church, and why it is important to think about an identity more broadly defined as "Christian" than "denominational," while recognizing that we who define ourselves in such ways are not the only Christians. You will learn of people who struggled with the meaning of history itself and asked what it means to participate in the mission of God in the world. You will meet people who valued their encounters with God's grace and presence in the context of worship. And you will see just how much Disciples through time have understood ministry itself to be connected not to an office or an administration or a particular church or denomination, but to all the people of God. In short, in these pages you will discover something of what it means to be Christian. That result alone just might provide all of us with a worthwhile reason to pray for the survival of something like denominations and for accessible treatments of their histories.

Mark G. Toulouse

Emmanuel College of Victoria University in
the University of Toronto

# Introduction

THE RELIGIOUS MOVEMENT THAT gave birth to the Christian
Church (Disciples of Christ) burst forth on the American frontier
early in the nineteenth century. This fact is important if we are to
understand the story of who the Disciples are and what they value.
What has come to be known as the Stone-Campbell Movement
was marked from the beginning by a frontier ethos of freedom,
anti-institutionalism, and individualism. You might say that this
is a denominational tradition with a libertarian streak. In addition
to its frontier ethos, the movement has been marked by its roots
in the Reformed tradition, for the founders of the movement were
first Presbyterians before taking the steps that led to the creation
of a new American religious movement. While Disciples are heirs
of the Reformed tradition, they, along with the other two major
branches of the Stone-Campbell Movement, are marked by their
points of resistance. This is especially true regarding demands for
doctrinal conformity. As a result, Disciples take pride in being a
non-creedal tradition.

The Stone-Campbell Movement, of which the Disciples are
but one branch, saw itself as an attempt at re-envisioning Christianity for a new century (the nineteenth century). Freed from the
bonds of inherited tradition, it would chart a new course that would
unite Christians everywhere in an evangelistic mission that would
touch the world. The foundation for this effort was to be found in

the pages of the New Testament. Freedom, unity, evangelism, and restorationism would be hallmarks of this new movement.

Two important events served to form the identity of the Stone-Campbell Movement. The first event was Barton Stone's participation in the Cane Ridge Revival of 1801, along with his subsequent break from the Presbyterian Church over theological differences. Secondly, the Scottish Presbyterian minister Thomas Campbell issued the *Declaration and Address* in 1809, in which he laid out his vision of a movement of unity among Christians. The first event links the movement to the outbreak of the Second Great Awakening, putting the movement in the middle of an effort to evangelize the new nation. The second served as a call to unity among Christians in the service of this task of evangelization. By leaving behind outworn beliefs and practices, these pioneer reformers believed, the church would be more effective in reaching the large numbers living outside the bounds of the church. In other words, the *why* of this new movement of reform was evangelism. Living on the frontier of a new nation, the founders of this movement sought to make the Christian message relevant to a new age.

Much has changed since the early nineteenth century, but in many ways the Disciples continue to be a frontier people. Freed from the encumbrances of rigid traditions and rules, frontier people must adapt to their surroundings, making do with what they have at their disposal. Even if the Christian Church (Disciples of Christ) that exists today has become fully integrated into mainstream denominational Protestant Christianity, it is marked by unease with hierarchy, rigid traditions, and cumbersome rules. In theory, this is a denominational tradition built for an age when growing numbers of people are questioning the value of institutional religion.

As a Christian communion, Disciples trace their heritage to the reforming impulses of several figures, all of whom came out of the Presbyterian tradition. Three were immigrants and one was frontier born. They include Thomas Campbell (1763–1854), his son Alexander (1788–1866), Barton Stone (1772–1844), and Walter Scott (1796–1861). Although all four men began their ministries as Presbyterians, they chose to strike out in pursuit of Christian unity, hoping that their efforts would bring unity to the churches and out of that the evangelization of the world. Indeed, all four men were committed to uniting Protestant churches in the United States along biblical principles so that God's kingdom might be established on earth. That same impulse remains at the center of the tradition, as is seen in the denominational mission statement: "We are a movement of wholeness in a fragmented world."

As a pastor of Disciples churches I have come to believe that it is important that we gain a clear understanding of our ethos and values as a denomination. With that in mind I offered a series of sermons at First Christian Church of Santa Barbara that lifted up what I considered to be the core values of our tradition. I chose to repeat this effort in each of the two congregations I later served as pastor. In this book I seek to share the essence of those efforts, though in expanded form, in the hope that other Disciples congregations might have the opportunity to reflect on our common values and practices in pursuit of the upward call of God. What I am sharing are, you might say, what I believe to be the pillars of our common tradition.

In the course of creating this book the ideas first shared in these sermons have been revised and expanded. My hope is that in reading this book, and discussing it together as congregations, both lifelong Disciples and inquirers into the Disciples tradition will discover what it means to be a Disciple. By understanding our identity as a community of faith we can catch the vision—the *why*—that undergirds the existence of Disciple congregations. Likewise, my hope is that those of us who belong to these congregations might better understand how belonging to these communities contributes to our journey as followers of Jesus Christ in the twenty-first century.

In seeking to understand our denominational identity, it is important that we as Disciples acknowledge our tendency to see the world and the Christian faith in an ahistorical fashion. That is, our restorationist impulses (wanting to return to the earliest, supposedly pristine, era of the tradition) have at times blinded us to the resources that the traditions of historic Christianity can bring to our faith journey. This tendency is, in my mind as a church historian, unfortunate. Our ahistorical attitudes have also impeded our appreciation of our own Stone-Campbell history and the resources present in it. If we are to face the future with both confidence and with humility it will be important, indeed essential, that we reclaim our identity—an identity that has been forged by those who went before us.

The six-week sermon series upon which much of the book is based was inspired by my reading of Mark Toulouse's thematic history of the Disciples, *Joined in Discipleship: The Shaping of Contemporary Disciple Identity* (Chalice, 1997). It should be consulted for a deeper understanding of the Disciple ethos and tradition. As a body of people who are free in Christ, I have discerned six core values or principles that define the movement we call the Christian Church (Disciples of Christ). Understanding these values can help guide us as we move into the future.

It is my hope that the reader will find these words beneficial in understanding who the Christian Church (Disciples of Christ) is, knowing that we are truly a product of our history. By understanding the history and theology of the movement, we will be in a better position to reclaim our identity as a movement of reform and unity, and become the people God has called us to be.

# 1

# Disciples Set Free

YEARS AGO I ATTENDED a Disciples seminarians conference. During one of the sessions a seminarian from Harvard reported that the Disciples of Christ as a denomination was an unknown entity in New England. In fact, most people in that part of the country seemed to think that his denomination was some kind of exotic cult. Now, I've never thought of the Disciples as either exotic or cultic, but of course it doesn't really matter what I think about my denominational home. Even if I don't think of the Disciples as cultic, it's quite possible that outside our own circle people could get the impression that we are a rather odd bunch. Perhaps it's because I've never lived in the Disciples heartland that I have found it necessary to regularly explain who the Disciples are. While my questioners are often good Protestant Christians, they seem to have little knowledge of my tribe. They know who the Presbyterians and the Baptists are, but as for the Disciples, we are an unknown quantity. This seems to be as true in Michigan and California as it is in New England.

There was a time when I could count myself among those who didn't know anything about the Disciples of Christ. That is due to the fact that I'm not a lifelong Disciple and didn't encounter Disciples churches until I enrolled in a Disciples-related college after high school. Before I became a member of the Christian Church (Disciples of Christ), I had been an Episcopalian and a Pentecostal. Even since my first embrace of the Disciples as a college student,

I've sojourned with several other denominations. Despite my religious wanderings, I have found a home among the Disciples.

So, why am I a Disciple? What attracted me to this tribe and kept me a member of the tribe? The answer can be found in the core values that define the movement's identity. I've come to appreciate these values, especially its witness to the importance of Christian unity. I also have embraced its affirmation of the New Testament witness to the lordship of Jesus and the longstanding commitment to the principle of freedom, especially as it regards to the interpretation of Scripture.

## A Commitment to Christian Unity

We have often used Barton Stone's metaphor of the polar star to describe the Disciples emphasis on Christian unity, but one could ask whether the pursuit of Christian unity truly stands at the center of the Disciples' life. Are we truly committed to unity as our founding vision? Ronald Osborn spoke of the need for Disciples not to evade our vocation, but to affirm that despite our schisms we "believe that God wills the oneness of his people" and "that emphasis on Jesus Christ provides the basis for Christian unity with the widest range of diversity and freedom."[1]

The founding pastor of the congregation that I currently serve, Edgar DeWitt Jones, was a committed ecumenist, both locally and nationally. He strongly affirmed this vocation to pursue unity. Not only did he participate in local ecumenical efforts and provide leadership to the denomination's ecumenical agencies, he served as President of the Federal Council of Churches (the predecessor of the National Council of Churches). In a sermon he preached, perhaps in the early 1940s, entitled "A Personal Confession of Faith," Jones declared:

> Progressively interpreted, the Disciples of Christ embody
> a noble plea and an arresting program. They cherish the
> dream of a reunited church, and make Christ central in

1. Osborn, *Experiment in Liberty*, 106.

teaching and in life. They emphasize unity but not uniformity. It is a roomy fellowship, holding to a universal
creed: "I believe in Christ as the Son of God and my personal Savior."[2]

It is this commitment to Christian unity that Jones exemplified
in his own ministry that drew me to the Disciples. The Disciples
seemed like a natural fit, considering my own faith journey, which
has run the gamut from Episcopalian to Pentecostal. When I joined
up with the Disciples I was looking for a tradition that would allow
me to retain much from my rather mixed bag of faith experiences.
What is true for me seems to be true of many others I've met over
the years.

The Disciples commitment to unity is rooted in the experiences of the founders with frontier Christianity in the early years
of the nineteenth century. It was a time when most Christians not
only believed that their brand of Christianity was the only accept-
able version, but they were known fight with each other, often calling each other names that would make modern politicians blush.
It was in that context that the Campbells and Barton Stone asked
the question: If we as Christians claim to follow Jesus and affirm
the Bible, why are we divided?

Thomas Campbell called the divisions among Christians a
"horrid evil" and "anti-Christian." Barton Stone spoke of the divisions among Christians as "drinking up the spirits of the godly,
destroying the influence of Christianity, and barring the way to
heaven."[3] That sense of calling has fueled the Disciples movement
to this day, even if we've had our share of divisions. Our history
records two major breaks, leading to the existence of three major
branches of the Stone-Campbell Movement.[4] Our commitment to
Christian unity can be seen in the fact that although we're a rather
small denomination, we've produced a significant number of important ecumenical leaders, including Paul Crow, the first general

2. Jones, *A Man Stood Up to Preach*, 190.

3. Stone, "To the Church Scattered," 162.

4. See Dunnavant et al., *Founding Vocation*, for a helpful discussion of how
the three denominations emerged from the founding vision.

secretary of the Consultation on Church Union; Michael Kinnamon, who served as general secretary of three unity organizations, the Consultation on Church Union, Churches Uniting in Christ, and the National Council of Churches; and Richard Hamm, who served as the executive director of another broader coalition of Christians, Christian Churches Together. If you take a close look at the history of the ecumenical movement over the past century, you will find Disciples featured prominently among the participants and the leaders.

Unfortunately, our witness to unity gets diluted when we begin to think that unity equals uniformity. Although uniformity may make unity easier to achieve, such a narrow vision doesn't accomplish the goal of uniting a diverse body of Christians together in Christ. Our witness as Disciples is this: We can be of one mind in Christ without agreeing with each other on every issue! Therefore, if we keep working on the task of unity, then we'll be true to our calling as Disciples. And as the psalmist puts it: "How good and pleasant it is, when kindred live together in unity" (Ps 133:1). Indeed!

## A New Testament Witness to Jesus Christ

If unity is the Disciples' polar star, then the question remains: On what basis do we unite? Our founders believed that when we get hung up on boundary issues—rules, regulations, and doctrines—we will end up dividing over them. If we focus instead on the New Testament witness to Jesus Christ, then we will find our source of unity. This hasn't proven to be an easy road to trod, but the founders believed that the best course of action was to embrace Peter's summarization of the gospel: "You are the Christ, the Son of the Living God." They concluded that if this confession was good enough for Jesus, then surely it is good enough for modern Christians!

There is simplicity to this Good Confession, but it leaves many people wanting a more precise definition. They are concerned about the substance of that claim. The statement itself is broad enough that it gives a great degree of freedom to define the meaning of who Jesus is and how we relate to God through him. For those who want to have a degree of certainty about the truth inherent in the confession, this broadness can be troubling. Of course, the question of truthfulness is an important one. As Jesus said: "You will know the truth and the truth will make you free" (John 8:32). Disciples have always believed that this liberating truth is to be found in Jesus, even if not in specific belief statements about him. There is an assumption that beliefs about God and Jesus and the Holy Spirit have evolved over time. For many Disciples, the focus is less on doctrinal definition and more on living out the moral and ethical teachings of Jesus. The message is simple, but it's not simplistic. Instead of placing the emphasis on boundaries, Disciples have generally focused on the center, allowing the boundaries to take care of themselves.

## Call to Freedom

If unity is the polar star and guiding force of this movement, it is set in the context of freedom. There is common agreement that Christians have been called upon to unite around a common confession that Jesus is the Messiah and the Son of the Living God. If this confession is to be transformative, however, it cannot be coerced. It has to be freely chosen. It should not surprise anyone that such a belief would emerge in a movement that formed soon after the birth of a nation that promised freedom of religion. The message of the founders was that each believer had the freedom to read and interpret the biblical text for themselves.

As a movement born on the American frontier just decades after the founding of the American nation, freedom was in the air as Barton Stone and Thomas Campbell began their ministries of reformation, animating new visions and opportunities for Christians to experiment with new organizational forms and theological perspectives. Freed from government and even denominational restrictions and interference, churches of all kinds sprung up on the frontier. Competition was the order of day, along with theological heterodoxy. In some ways, spiritual anarchy ruled the day! It was in the midst of this increasingly chaotic context, which produced movements such as the Mormons and the Shakers, that the Stone-Campbell Movement, out of which the Disciples emerged, was born.

The founders came to believe that it was essential that people have the freedom to read, interpret, and apply Scripture for themselves. With this in mind, they questioned the authority of creeds and religious hierarchies. At the same time, they encouraged laypersons to take control of their own spiritual lives. They communicated this message through sermons, debates, newspapers, and books. Just as blogs offer people today the opportunity to share a message to a broad audience, newspapers did the same for that generation. It was often said that although the Disciples didn't have bishops, they did have many editors! These editors and preachers encouraged everyone, whether preacher or layperson, male or female, to educate themselves so they could effectively interpret the texts of Scripture.

It is important to note that the earliest Disciples colleges were not designed to train clergy. They were founded by reformers who hoped to provide all Christians with the necessary tools for reading, understanding, and interpreting the Bible, even as they prepared for careers outside the church. In time educational institutions, including seminaries, were established to provide the churches with an educated (and even professional) ministry.

Due to the fact that this new religious movement reflected the cultural and social dynamics of the age, it was in a good position to grow quickly. It worked because people were hungry for the opportunity to think for themselves about the things of God. Yes, it could be messy at times, but the results were powerful.

This exuberance didn't last forever. In part, this is because many Christians concluded that it's easier to let someone else do the difficult work of interpreting Scripture than take responsibility for their own spiritual lives. Even within this movement that cherishes its freedom to interpret and apply Scripture, biblical illiteracy is rampant.

Biblical illiteracy persists in our churches even though a majority of church people claim that they believe in the teachings of the Bible. Because Disciples are a non-creedal people, this is an unfortunate situation. If "we have no creed but Christ, and no book but the Bible," it is vitally important to know the story of Jesus. If we do not know the story then we will not know who we are or what we are about. Indeed, when we do not know the story it is more likely that our faith will be defined by the surrounding culture than the ethos of the Christian faith.

Considering this problem of biblical illiteracy in Disciples churches, it might be helpful to remember the words of St. Augustine (even if Disciples tend not to be followers of the great fourth-century theologian), who spoke of the Christian journey in terms of "faith seeking understanding." Having the freedom to choose one's beliefs requires that one take responsibility for understanding the content of those beliefs. The pursuit of understanding is, of course, a lifelong journey.

If Disciples were to take hold of the principle of Christian freedom, and begin to live it out with enthusiasm, then this movement would have an important gift to offer the church at large. Indeed, it would possess a gift for all those in the world who are seeking after spiritual things in an environment that allows room for dissent. The question is: What will it mean to embrace this principle of liberty that so clearly defines the Disciples identity?

A number of years ago Ronald Osborn, a noted Disciple historian and church leader, wrote a book entitled *Experiment in Liberty*. In it Osborn named several freedoms he believed should define the Disciples identity. I believe that these freedoms commend themselves to the current age.

## *You Have the Freedom to Respond to the Gospel*

God has not determined your fate. You have freedom to choose your own life path. In other words, your decision to follow the gospel is not predetermined or predestined. While the movement has Reformed roots, Disciples have largely affirmed the principle that God's grace provides room for humans to cooperate with God (or not) in accomplishing God's will. That includes one's ultimate destiny.[5] Even as God does not determine one's future, neither does the government, one's family, or one's culture. All of these may have an influence, but in the end each one has the opportunity to say yes or no to God's call. One can choose to follow the way of Jesus or not—again, that is a choice one has the freedom to make.

## *You Are Free from Creedalism.*

Even as one can say either yes or no to God's invitation to join the family, Disciples do not have an officially sanctioned creed or statement of faith that one must affirm as a requirement for membership in the community. While Disciples do not require adherence to a statement of faith, including the historic creeds, this does not mean that creeds don't have any value for Disciples as resources for Christian growth. The most recent Disciples hymnal includes several faith statements, including the Apostles' Creed and the Nicene Creed, along with the Preamble to *The Design of the Christian Church (Disciples of Christ)*. This Preamble takes the form of a theological confession that gives voice to the Disciples vision of God, the church, and the world.

Disciples theologian Ralph Wilburn makes the distinction between a *confessing* church and a *confessionalist* church. The latter is a church that considers "*its own confession* as an ultimate, while a *confessing* church is one that "confesses Jesus Christ as Lord, listens continuously to hear his word, and to learn its relevance to concrete situations in existence."[6] Creeds have value to the church by offering a witness to what the historic church has considered important. They provide a community-based witness concerning difficult theological points, such as the nature of God and the person of Jesus, but they are not the last word that puts to an end

---

5. Two contemporary theological movements that resonate with the Disciples are open theism and process theology. On open theism see Pinnock, *Most Moved Mover*; on process theology see Epperly, *Process Theology*.

6. Wilburn, "Lordship of Jesus Christ," 186–87.

further conversation. Most Disciples churches simply require that candidates for baptism and membership make the same confession that Peter made to Jesus: "you are the Christ, the son of the living God" (Matt 16:16).

## You Are Free from Ignorance and Superstition.

The Disciples have often been called a rationalist sect. That is because Disciples have long valued the life of the mind. That shouldn't be surprising for a movement that looked to John Locke and other Enlightenment figures for its philosophical grounding. Locke was a strong proponent of a simple and reasonable Christianity, and the founders followed this vision in embracing a reasonable or rational reading of the Scriptures, which they believed were foundational to reforming the church. They believed that the reform of Christianity required a community of believers who were sufficiently grounded in Scripture that they could read it, understand it, and follow its teachings in life.

Because the founders held human reason in high regard, they started schools and colleges so that everyone, whether preacher or businessperson, could have a deep introduction not only to the Bible—including the study of Greek and Hebrew—but also the liberal arts and the sciences. This is because they believed that any Christian (at least any male Christian), if called upon, should be able to mount the steps of the pulpit and preach.

With this in mind, Alexander Campbell offered his students and the readers of his books and journals principles of biblical interpretation insisting that we should read the Bible just like we read every other book. The Bible may be a sacred book, but it is still a book. Since reason played such an important role in Campbell's understanding of faith, he encouraged his followers to study not only the Bible, but also modern science, history, and linguistics. It's okay to be emotional and to trust yourself to God, but just remember: You can't be free if you don't think for yourself.

*You Are Free from the Law of Sin and Death.*

This fourth point is important because it deals with the spiritual life of the Christian. If you live your life in relationship to the God revealed in Jesus Christ, then there is no need to fear death. Your past does not determine your future. Osborn wrote that "in offering deliverance from guilt, it releases the Christian from the burden of a troubled conscience, putting to an end alienation from God and neighbor."[7] As good Lockeans, the founding generation rejected the idea of original sin. Humans are born with a blank slate, and therefore are not programmed to sin. Sin is a choice, not a curse. Because Christ frees us from our accumulated bondage to sin, we can start life anew. Freedom is a wonderful gift, but we must remember that freedom presents its own set of dangers. If not lived responsibly, freedom can lead to chaos.

There is an old saying that was once popular in Disciples circles: "We're not the only Christians, just Christians only." As a community of faith living within the greater body of Christ, we have a special gift to bring to the world. We may not be a creedal people, but we do have strong set of core values that help define our identity as a people. These values include a commitment to Christian unity and that is rooted in an embrace of the spiritual freedom of every person. These, and other values that we will name, are worth celebrating and embodying!

7. Osborn, *Experiment in Liberty*, 58.

# 2

# Personal Freedom and
# Biblical Interpretation

THE YEAR 2009 MARKED the bicentennial of the publication of Thomas Campbell's *Declaration and Address*. When Campbell issued his declaration in 1809 from the American frontier (western Pennsylvania), the Campbell side of the Stone-Campbell Movement was born. We are used to thinking of the frontier beginning west of the Mississippi, but in 1809 the edge of the frontier still lay relatively close to the eastern coast of the United States. Frontier life offered people the opportunity to break free of older traditions and institutions. As the Second Great Awakening rolled across the American landscape at the beginning of the nineteenth century, people living on the frontier began weighing whether they wanted to stay with their traditions or instead embrace new understandings of religion. It was a time of great spiritual upheaval and experimentation, with movements as diverse as the Church of Jesus Christ of Latter Day Saints and the Shakers taking form. There was also the option of walking away completely from institutional forms of religion. In that there are many similarities between the early nineteenth century and the early twenty-first century.

It was in the midst of this religious ferment that the Stone-Campbell Movement emerged. Thomas Campbell, a Presbyterian pastor who had recently emigrated from Scotland, became disturbed not only by the confusion, but also by the unwillingness of his colleagues to entertain the thought that this disunity might not be in accord with the wisdom and will of God. In response, he began preaching a message of unity that he believed was rooted in the New Testament. He told the people living on the frontier that they didn't need human creeds to interpret the gospel; they simply needed to allow the Bible to speak to them anew. Campbell also tried to elevate the position of the laity to one of equality with the clergy in spiritual matters. The laity were not just leaders in the church, they were in truth ministers of the gospel.

The movement grew quickly on the frontier, largely because it wasn't traditionalist and was flexible and responsive to its environment. It even had a little of Daniel Boone and Davey Crockett in it. After all, one of the earliest Disciples preachers went by the name of Raccoon John Smith. This was a faith fit for the journey west. You might even say it was the missional movement of the early nineteenth century. While the missional concept has become popular with many contemporary Disciples churches, it was already in the genetic code of the movement.[1]

## Embracing the Interpretation Principle?

Among the principles and values that emerged out of this frontier ferment was something that Mark Toulouse has called the "interpretation principle."[2] What is the interpretation principle? When we make the comment that something is "a matter of interpretation," what we mean to say is that there is more than one way of looking at it. That includes the biblical story. It's like figuring out the color of the paint on the wall. Is it purple or plum? Eggplant or violet? Of course, figuring out the meaning of Scripture has

---

1. Although I want to celebrate this frontier/pioneering spirit present in the early Disciples movements, I'm also reminded by Sandhya Jha that in their westward vision the Disciples essentially ignored non-white persons present in North America, including Hispanics, Asians, and Native Americans. Jha, *Room at the Table*, 6–7.

2. Toulouse, *Joined In Discipleship*, 37–53.

considerably more implications than determining the color of the paint on the living room wall.

When people ask questions about my church, they will often ask what we believe about the Bible. What they're looking for is a sense of our theological starting point. My answer to that question often makes the person asking the question uncomfortable. That's because I try to steer the discussion away from questions of biblical authority toward biblical interpretation.[3]

When it comes to interpreting the Bible, I tell inquirers that the responsibility for doing this task belongs to the individual Christian. In the Disciples tradition, individuals have the freedom to read, interpret, and apply the Scriptures for themselves. There are no creeds, statements of faith, or hierarchies that determine the way in which a person must read and understand the words they find in the Bible. While this "interpretation principle" assumes individual freedom, it must be tempered by the recognition that the most responsible way of interpreting the Bible is to learn from others, including those who are specially trained in these matters.

While it should be remembered that one of the causes of division within the Stone-Campbell Movement was the growing influence of the historical-critical method of biblical study in Disciples circles at the turn of the twentieth century, and that many of our current conflicts within the church center on the weight we give to critical scholarship, giving attention to biblical scholarship is an important check on our tendency toward private interpretation. Unfortunately, critical scholarship is too often not shared with congregations in a way that enables them to engage Scripture in a way that is both responsible and faith-forming. This engagement needs to be accompanied by a reaffirmation of biblical authority, even as we reject biblical literalism. It will also need to be accompanied by an effort to overcome biblical illiteracy.[4]

While tradition was often deemed irrelevant among earlier generations of Disciples, it provides a check on private

3. On the question of biblical authority, I have presented my own understanding in my *Authority of the Bible in a Postmodern Age*.

4. Boring, *Disciples and the Bible*, 417–27.

interpretation as well. As Disciples historical theologian William Tabbernee suggests, "for contemporary Disciples, this means (despite the earlier often misunderstood rhetoric against 'creeds') getting to know, and taking seriously, the Apostolic Tradition(s) *as well as* the Bible." He writes further: "as Disciples, we ultimately decide what we believe (i.e., 'our theology') 'for ourselves' . . . but we do not decide what we believe '*by* ourselves.'"[5] That distinction is often ignored, but it is an important qualifier for defining one's freedom in the process of interpretation. Responsible interpretation is not private interpretation; it is interpretation done in conversation with critical scholarship, tradition, and the broader community.

When the principle was first formulated, the founding generation was influenced by an Enlightenment confidence that, when approached from the standpoint of reason, the biblical text is sufficiently clear so that its meaning can be understood without external forms of guidance. This confidence can be misplaced, especially since Scripture isn't quite as clear in its pronouncements as some thought. In spite of the risks, there were many who embraced the opportunity to take control of the interpretive process. Others, however, found this form of freedom quite frightening. While the founding generation may have been overly optimistic about the clarity of the text, by taking this step they empowered the laity to take control of the interpretive process for themselves (if not by themselves).

While some people might be frightened by having so much freedom to read and experience the Christian faith as it is laid out in Scripture, there have always been those who find this approach to faith both inviting and refreshing. Of course, this freedom of interpretation not only can make things interesting; it can make church life a bit chaotic at times. Those who find this freedom inviting often do so because it respects one's ability, when guided by the Spirit of God and the use of reason and tradition (Disciples might be more comfortable with the word "history," but "tradition" is the better term), to understand Scripture and apply it faithfully.

5. Tabbernee, "Theology and Tradition," 53.

Church conflicts often emerge when people refuse to grant to their neighbors the same freedoms they desire for themselves. If we are willing to respect the opinions of others, allowing them the same freedoms we covet for ourselves, then even when we disagree we can find unity in a common faith in Christ. This was, I believe, the desire of Jesus and of our Disciples founders.

If we are going to successfully navigate our way through the challenges posed by freedom of interpretation, then it is necessary that we recognize that unity does not mean uniformity. In a community that values freedom, participants must allow for the presence of differences of belief and practice. Indeed, participation in what some have called "communities of conversation" requires readiness to live with some degree of discomfort. In this regard, Ronald J. Allen, himself a Disciple, writes:

> The blunt fact is that conversation sometimes leads to discomfort. Nevertheless, naming the causes of such discomfort can be an important part of the encounter with the other. Not only does it bring honesty to the conversation but it can provoke us to recognize and claim things about ourselves we need to face.[6]

When we seek to live as a community of conversation, it is not simply a matter of agreeing to disagree. Instead, it requires that we learn to listen respectfully to each other, while recognizing the right and responsibility of the other to pursue the truth that is God.

This is an important point, because in 2 Timothy, a letter perhaps written by Paul, but more likely a later follower of Paul, we are reminded that Scripture not only gives us information about God, it provides an important foundation for the journey of faith. We are told that Scripture is "useful for teaching, for reproof, for correction, and for training in righteousness, so that everyone who belongs to God may be proficient, equipped for every good work" (2 Tim 3:16–17). So how do we experience the practical implications of our encounter with the Bible?

---

6. Allen, "Church as a Community," 489–91.

## *Being Clear About Our Assumptions Concerning the Bible*

Although Disciples do not have creeds, we do have some wonderful slogans that remind us to take the Bible seriously. One of these slogans declares: "We have no Creed but Christ, no Book but the Bible." Another one proclaims: "Where the Scriptures speak we speak, where the Scriptures are silent we are silent." What these slogans suggest to us is that a person's own interpretation cannot have priority over that of another person. It also means that the essentials of the Christian faith should be few in number, for in essentials we are to be unified, while in nonessentials there is room for difference.

What is the purpose of the Bible? According to what we read in 2 Timothy 3, Scripture is inspired by God and is "useful for teaching, for reproof, for correction, and for training in righteousness." The Bible that the author of the letter has in mind is the Hebrew Bible (Old Testament). Having been provided this instruction and correction, the people of God are "equipped for every good work" (2 Tim 3:16–17). As I read a text like this, I'm led to believe that God uses Scripture to inform and equip the people of God to live lives of purpose and service in God's creation. So, when we go to Scripture seeking to hear from God, what is it that we should expect to hear? In what way does the Bible bring us the Word of God?

Did God dictate it? If the Bible is perfect, without error, then how did God make sure this happened? Very few Christians would affirm the premise that God dictates the very words we read in Scripture. If God doesn't dictate the words of the Bible, then what should we make of words that come to us through the hands and minds of human beings who lived at least nineteen hundred years ago? How can they communicate to us a word from God? If we affirm the human authorship of Scripture, then surely it must reflect the limitations imposed by human language, history, and experience. Indeed, this must be true of the authors and the original readers/hearers of these words. Their worldviews and experiences were very different from ours, and yet if we are willing to listen to the voices present in Scripture, then perhaps God can speak to us through their words.

When it comes to reading and applying the words of Scripture, I believe we must come to this task with a deep sense of humility. That is because Christians don't usually divide over questions of biblical authority; they divide over the interpretation of the Bible (even if the partisans in the debate assume it's a matter of authority).

I've heard it said of me that I don't believe in the Bible. My accusers say this because my interpretation of Scripture differs from theirs. Of course, I'm not alone in this. Perhaps you have had it said about you as well. So, what does this mean? If you listen closely, you discover that what someone means by this is that they don't read the Bible in the same way you do. That often leads to the conclusion that your reading is wrong, deficient, and perhaps even heretical. Of course this goes both ways. I might think the same way about someone else's interpretation.

When we get in conversations like this, it is important to remember that the texts we're talking about were written centuries ago, in languages few of us read today, to people whose worldviews were often very different from our own. While Disciples take the Scriptures as a norm, even as the normative theological source, it is important that we recognize the incompleteness of our own understanding of the text. If Disciples are committed to Christian unity, then we will need to give each other room to hear, interpret, and apply this word to one's own life.

If we're going to do this successfully, then we must check our assumptions before we come to the Scriptures. We need to ask ourselves—much like a Supreme Court Justice, at least in my mind, should before reading the Constitution—the following questions: What are my life experiences, biases, and ideologies? How might they affect the way I read this text? After all, I am a well-educated, white, middle-class, middle-aged male living in the early twenty-first century in the United States of America, which at this moment is understood to be the lone superpower in the world. I have to ask how my identity colors the way I read the text of Scripture.

I'd like to believe that I'm immune from such biases, but I'm not. That doesn't mean that any and all interpretations are equally valid (Disciples are rooted in a vision formed by the Enlightenment that highly valued human reason), it's just that we must keep our own contexts in mind as we try to travel back to a different time and place so we can hear a word from God in these texts.

If we are to faithfully live out the Christian faith, with Scripture as our guide, then it would behoove us to humbly consider how the life experiences of our neighbors might color their interpretation. For example, how might an impoverished farmer living in Sub-Saharan Africa read Scripture? How might he hear a text such as the parable of the sower? Or what about a woman living in one of Rio's favelas (slums)? How might she hear the prophet speak judgment on the oppressor (Isa 10:1–4)? Or how might someone living in the religiously and ethnically diverse cultures of India hear a text suggesting that Jesus is the only way of salvation (Acts 4:12)? How will such persons read and interpret these texts in their own life contexts? Indeed, as a male I need to ask how a woman might read a text that suggests that women should submit to or obey a man.

One of the issues that currently roils the waters of the Christian community concerns the way we should read texts that seem to deal with same-gender intimacy. Many, including myself, have argued that there are important differences in understanding that separate the ancient world and the modern world. If our cultural and social dynamics do not match that of the ancient world, how should we read texts that are challenged by current societal norms? It is possible that we should follow the lead of our ancient ancestors, but as we have discerned with slavery and (for most Disciples) with the roles of women in church and society, current norms require us to re-evaluate the way we read and apply Scripture.

## Following the General Rules of Literary
## Interpretation When Reading the Bible

If we start the process of reading the Bible responsibly by looking inward and examining our own biases and context, then the next step is to focus our attention on the text itself. With this in mind, Alexander Campbell offers us a set of interpretive principles. He wrote in the *Millennial Harbinger* (1832) that "if then God speaks in human language, must not his communications be submitted to the same rules of interpretation as all other verbal communication?"[7] The Bible may be sacred to us, but when we read it, shouldn't we use the same principles and tools that we would use to read and understand any other piece of literature? Wouldn't this be especially true when we're dealing with a piece of literature that is at least two thousand years old and was written in languages very different from our own?

Reading the Bible responsibly means taking into consideration the historical, cultural, and literary context of the passage. I can't just sit down, open to a page, and read it as if it was written yesterday with me in mind. Christians can't just sit down with the Hebrew Bible and read Christian theology into it, without first asking what the original hearers of this word would have heard. Yes, if we're going to hear a word from God from this book, then we have some hard work to do.

If we're willing to take the time to read the Bible responsibly, using the best tools at hand, then I believe we can experience the presence of the living God in its pages. Fortunately some of the hard work has already been done for us by modern Bible translators. They have already started the interpretive process by translating the Hebrew and Greek into a language we can read and understand. Beyond our translations, it is helpful to consult a Bible dictionary or commentary.[8] I think this is what Alexander

---

7. Campbell quoted in Toulouse, *Joined in Discipleship*, 41.

8. We are blessed by a large number of biblical commentaries written by Disciples scholars, including the very accessible one-volume commentary titled *The People's New Testament Commentary*, written by Boring and Craddock.

Campbell meant when he wrote that "the Bible reading of all enlightened Christians generally terminates in a Sacred dialogue between the author and the reader."[9] For Campbell, authorship is somehow shared by the human writer and the God who inspired the words written on the page. In essence, Campbell is inviting us to listen in on a conversation between biblical author and the Holy Spirit, with the expectation that in the end we will be equipped to engage in good works.

## Recognizing the Limitations of Private Interpretation

While it is liberating to hear that we are free to read, interpret, and apply the Scriptures for ourselves, what does that mean in practice? What does it mean that no one has the authority—not even a preacher—to tell a person how they must read and interpret a text?

When Alexander Campbell introduced this principle of interpretation in the nineteenth century, it was believed by many that the Scriptures had sufficient clarity that the unimpeded reader might discover the truth embedded in them. They looked to philosophers like John Locke and Thomas Reid (from Scotland), who insisted that in most cases we can trust common sense. This Enlightenment ideal is best expressed in that famous phrase from the Declaration of Independence: "We hold these truths to be self-evident, that all men are created equal, that they are endowed by their Creator with certain unalienable Rights, that among these are Life, Liberty and the pursuit of Happiness."

When Thomas Jefferson spoke of "self-evident truths," how self-evident were they? It would appear that Jefferson didn't believe that everyone living on American soil was created equal. I don't think he included women or people of color in his definition, nor did he believe that his slaves had unalienable rights. When we read the words of the Declaration of Independence today, do we read them in the same way Jefferson understood them, or do we read our own realities into them? If the Declaration of Independence

9. Campbell, quoted in Toulouse, *Joined in Discipleship*, 45

requires reinterpretation, then the same is likely true of Scripture. Its meaning might not be as clear as we'd like to think.

Having embraced this common-sense approach to Scripture, many participants in the Stone-Campbell Movement came to believe that if everyone let go of their inherited traditions and creeds, along with interpretations handed down by theologians and preachers throughout the centuries, then Christians would find the necessary common ground upon which to unite. It sounds easy enough, but when you actually try to do this it's pretty difficult. Indeed, in recent years we've discovered that the more freedom we have to interpret the text, the more varied the interpretations.

The Reformation served as a good example of what happens when you embrace the principle of *sola scriptura* ("Scripture alone"). A Pandora's box was opened, and everyone became their own pope, offering authoritative interpretations they expected others to embrace.

There is another complication that threatens our ability to interpret the Bible. It's one we've already encountered: the epidemic of biblical illiteracy in our churches. Huge swaths of the church do not know the basic narrative of the biblical story. In addition many have little understanding of the ancient world out of which these texts emerged. We read Romans 13, with its discussion of political authority, as if Paul was writing to people living in a twenty-first-century American democracy, when he was in fact writing to people living under what amounts to a dictatorship. Some emperors were better than others, but none of them were elected by or responsible to an electorate. It was to such a government that Paul encouraged obedience, and which he considered to have divinely given authority to keep the peace. Of course, it was this same government that crucified Jesus and later executed Paul.

There is also the rather personal way in which we read these texts. For example, if I were to tell a woman that she should remain silent in the church because that is what Paul told the women in the Corinthian church, she would likely object to this reading. That is, unless she has accepted this interpretation as having authority for today's women. What of Paul's encouragement to slaves that they should obey their masters? If I were a slave, would I hear this as being a word from God? Yes, there are many texts that can cause us trouble, texts that do not appear to bring to us a word from God. Consider those texts that suggest that God encourages genocide or that God disapproves of same-gender relationships. How do we deal with such texts in a way that is true to the original message and yet appropriate for our day?

You may have freedom to interpret the Bible, but if your interpretation affects my life in a way I deem inappropriate, then I likely will object to your interpretation. Of course, that is true of other documents, including the U.S. Constitution.

I can claim the freedom of interpretation, but surely there are limits to private interpretation. Paul offers a good word in this regard, reminding us that while all things might be lawful, not all things are profitable (1 Cor 10:23). I may be free to read Scripture for myself, but that doesn't mean that I can do whatever I please or impose my reading on other people without their consent. I would go so far as to suggest that not every interpretation of Scripture carries truth in it, nor is every interpretation beneficial to me or to the world. Yes, Paul's word to the Corinthians is quite applicable with regard to the way we read, interpret, and apply the words we encounter in the Bible.

## The Call to Responsible Interpretation

It is important to remember that people have used Scripture—I could say abused it—to support all kinds of evil. Slavery, segregation, the suppression of women, anti-Semitism, apartheid, and genocide are just a few of the horrors perpetrated by people who used the Bible to authorize their actions. We may be free, but we still need the community—both the church community and the community of scholars—to help guide us as we read and apply these words to our lives. Yes, we even need to hear the wisdom of tradition to guide us in our readings.[10]

10. The Campbells may have had their troubles with human traditions, which they considered divisive, but we might benefit from considering the

While it is important that we accord to others the same freedom that we wish to be accorded ourselves, there will be times when we feel it appropriate to offer a word of correction. When and if we do this, we should do so with humility and with the intent not to break fellowship. If we take the time to engage one another in conversation, then we might even discover that our own reading is incomplete or wrong. What the early leaders of the Stone-Campbell Movement, of which the Disciples are but one branch, insisted upon was that personal interpretations shouldn't be a test of fellowship.

One of the benefits as well as challenges of the modern age is that we have greater access to the text of Scripture than ever before. We live in a privileged age when the personal ownership of a Bible is quite common. However, not so long ago it was quite rare to own a Bible. Thus, most people depended on religious teachers for access to the biblical story. That is no longer true, at least not in America. Since the Bible is a perennial bestseller in America, I would guess that most American Christians have quite a collection of Bibles in their homes. Despite this unparalleled access to ownership of the Bible, including a myriad of new translations and study aids, surveys continue to report the news that most Americans are biblically illiterate.

If we are to embrace the "interpretation principle," then we must recover our biblical literacy. If we are to be true to our heritage then we must make, as Disciples Bible scholar Eugene Boring suggests, "an intentional decision to become a Bible-reading community of faith."[11] We can read it at home, in church, and in Bible studies. We can do it alone and with others. We can hear it read and expounded; we can debate it; and we can receive it as a gift from God. The good news is that we are free to read, interpret, and live this word from God in a community of support rather than one of condemnation.

way in which tradition, especially the consensus of the faithful, can help us broaden our understanding of the biblical witness. On tradition see Guarino, *Vincent of Lérins*, and Pelikan, *Vindication of Tradition*.

11. Boring, *Disciples and the Bible*, 426.

# 3

# Disciples and the Question of Authority

WHEN ARCHIE AND EDITH Bunker sat down at the piano and sang "Those Were the Days," they were engaging in a bit of nostalgia, pining for a time when life was simpler and more to their liking. It seems that every generation does the same. After all, I much prefer the Beatles to current musical offerings. When we reminisce, the days of our childhood seem simpler and more enjoyable than the present. I can remember my father talking fondly about growing up in upstate New York during the Great Depression. I think it was the movie and a burger for a quarter that stood out to him. Looking back to my own childhood, I might relish buying a Moody Blues album for less than four dollars or a sixteen-ounce bottle of soda for less than a quarter. Then there's the fun times playing whiffle ball in the meridian running down my street, or shoveling the snow off my neighbor's basketball court so we could play a bit of basketball. Yes, those were the days.

The preacher of Ecclesiastes might not agree with our reminiscences: "Do not say, 'Why were the former days better than these?' For it is not from wisdom that you ask this" (Eccl 7:10). We may be tempted to glorify the old days, but this will not lead us to God.

Nostalgia doesn't just affect individuals; it also affects institutions and communities. Churches have a tendency to pine for the good old days. "Remember," we ask our friends, "when the church was full and people were truly committed?" Or, "Do you remember the choir—how big and full it was?" Of course, we can't leave out the children's programs. "Wasn't it wonderful when all those children were running around? That was a grand scene, wasn't it?" You might even look back with fondness to the sermons preached by ministers of yesteryear. Yes, remember those good old days? If only we could turn back the clock, then everything would be as it should.

Church-related nostalgia can take one of two forms: traditionalism or primitivism. Traditionalism takes tradition, which historian Jaroslav Pelikan calls the "living faith of the dead," and hardens it into the "dead faith of the living."[1] We do things simply because that's the way we've always done them. Primitivism, on the other hand, assumes that the church has lost its way and we need to restore things to the way God intended them to be. Primitivists come in many forms, but each family of primitivists believes it has found the correct pathway home. Disciples have fallen prey to both of these temptations, but the one that has most defined us as a people is primitivism (also called restorationism).

There are branches of the Stone–Campbell Movement that still wear a Restorationist label, but most Disciples long ago abandoned restorationist language. While the Disciples share a common heritage with these Restorationist communions, by the mid-twentieth century most Disciples concluded that the idea of returning to a first-generation golden age was an illusion. There may be much to learn from the ancient church, but a critical reading of the New Testament failed to uncover a pristine church that could be restored in the present age. It was clear to many Disciples leaders that they could not simply turn back the clock to an earlier age and hope that by doing so the church would experience reformation and rebirth. There is another reason why Disciples abandoned restorationist language: the plea for restoration failed to deliver on its promise of bringing unity to the Christian community.

In spite of the Disciples' aversion to restorationist language and ideology, there is something about restorationism that is

1. Pelikan, *Vindication of Tradition*, 65.

attractive to Americans. We have this built-in desire to return to what Richard Hughes and Leonard Allen call "primal norms." If this is true, then perhaps we can reclaim something of this inheritance that continues to resonate with American religious and cultural life.[2]

## Restoration as Commitment to Biblical Faith

Some restorationists look to the New Testament, and especially the book of Acts, hoping to find there a blueprint of church order that can be reinstituted so as to ensure that we are faithful Christians. The unfortunate consequence of this is that it makes the institution (church offices and structures) the focus of our attention. If restoration of a specific biblical church order is seen as the foundation for Christian unity, then it becomes our creed. That seems like a rather odd emphasis for a movement that eschewed the creation of doctrinal creeds that would serve as a test of fellowship. Then again, institutional issues have often been the sticking point in ecumenical conversations.[3]

Blueprint restorationism falters when the New Testament is read with an open and critical mind. That is because the New Testament reveals a variety of ecclesial patterns. So, if we're going to restore the New Testament pattern of church order, which one is the correct version? Is it the free-flowing style of Corinth, or the orderly and somewhat traditionalist version described in the Pastoral Epistles?

If the search for the perfect church order is a rather quixotic effort, that does not mean there is nothing to gain from engaging with the book of Acts and the rest of the New Testament. If we approach the biblical story with a critical eye and an open heart, we can find perspectives and values that might inspire and assist

2. Hughes and Allen, *Illusions of Innocence*, 2–3.

3. See Watkins, *American Church*, 187–90, for a history of the Consultation on Church Union, where these conversations ultimately foundered not on theology or even sacramental understandings, but on questions of ministerial authority.

Disciples congregations in becoming a missional church for the twenty-first-century frontier. The book of Acts might not provide the blueprint for a perfect church, but the pages of Scripture do offer pictures of churches that adapted themselves to their environment, hoping that they could offer an effective and true witness to God's love for humanity. Certainly this is a vision of the church that we can restore.

While our engagement with the New Testament can instill a passion for mission that follows the example of first-century churches that adapted themselves to their various contexts, in affirming what Mark Toulouse has termed the "Restoration Principle" we also link ourselves to the mission envisioned by founders Barton Stone, the Campbells, and Walter Scott. That mission was rooted in the call to embody the message of Jesus in such a way that Christians might join together to share the good news of God's love for the world.

We go astray when we think that the New Testament is simply a set of principles for organizing an institution—principles that must be closely protected through the ages. If we wish to truly embrace the Restoration Principle, and with it our apostolic inheritance, then we must understand that it points us to the God who is revealed in the person of Jesus. This apostolic inheritance provides us with a lens through which we can examine our own history, traditions, and experiences with God. When we do this we can truly participate with Jesus in ministering in and with the world in which we live, bringing to it the blessings of God.

This apostolic inheritance is, at its root, the promise of a relationship with the church's founder, Jesus the Christ. Through his life and teachings, which have been interpreted and passed on to us by his followers through the pages of the New Testament, we can discover a pathway to God. This apostolic inheritance helps us discern God's will for the church so that it might "work and serve meaningfully in the midst of a hurting and broken world."[4]

4. Toulouse *Joined in Discipleship*, 57–58.

## Restorationism Gone Awry

Unfortunately, this principle can go awry when we begin to believe that we have reclaimed the "perfect and pristine church," or when we believe that we alone have discovered and restored the complete truth of God. It becomes a problem when the means becomes the end, or when we indulge in nostalgia and lose sight of what God is doing in our midst today. Over the years, we Disciples have fallen prey to this temptation for several reasons.

### We Developed Questionable Views of the Bible.

Things got messy when the founders began using American constitutional language as their lens for reading the Bible. Some became "strict constructionists," who read the Bible as if it were a law book. They turned narratives into propositions and proof texts upon which they could build systems. As they did this, many fell into legalism. Instead of being a word of freedom and grace, the Bible became a word of prohibition. Instead of offering a word of inclusion, it brought to the world a word of exclusion.

### We Developed Questionable Views of the Church.

This second problem stemmed from the first, because when we started reading the Bible as if it was the church's constitution, we began to think that we had found the institutional key to uniting the body of Christ. We got locked into a certain way of being church and forgot that a missional church must adapt to its environment. We forgot that the church is "rooted in its own historical and cultural setting and is, therefore, constantly changing and developing."[5] That was true in the first century, and it remains true to this day.

5. Ibid., 64.

## Restoring the Restoration Principle

So the question is: Can we reclaim the Restoration Principle, and if so, what would it look like in the twenty-first century? How can we restate it in a way that makes sense of our current situation? Turning again to Mark Toulouse, he offers four markers of the apostolic faith that stand out in Disciples thought. If we can reclaim them, then we will discover a way forward that is appropriate for us as Disciples.

### *The Confession of Christ as Son of God and Savior*

This is the confession of faith we make at our baptism and when we join with the church: "Jesus is the Christ, the Son of the Living God, and my Lord and Savior." This is our apostolic inheritance, for it is based on Matthew's account of Peter's confession, a confession that, according to the understanding of the early church, Jesus considered sufficient enough to build his church upon (Matt 16:16–18). It is also a simple and inclusive statement that allows for nuance and interpretation.

### *The Affirmation of the Holy Spirit's Guidance and Inspiration*

We make this affirmation by trusting the Spirit of God to work in our midst. In Acts 1, we hear Jesus telling the gathered disciples to wait for the Spirit, and then in Acts 2, we watch as the Spirit falls on the church, empowering the people of God to proclaim the gospel. The same can be true of us as well.[6] It is the Holy Spirit who continues to prod us on toward fulfilling God's purpose, which Disciples understand to be bringing unity to the body of Christ so that a fragmented world might experience wholeness and healing. In acknowledging the centrality of the Holy Spirit, it is important

---

6. On the role of the Spirit in empowering the church and the people of God to serve God in the world see Cornwall, *Unfettered Spirit*.

to note that, due to an inherent rationalism that has eschewed emotionalism in religious life, Disciples have often given the Holy Spirit short shrift.[7] In this regard, Alexander Campbell tended to equate the Holy Spirit with the Bible. Nonetheless, in the New Testament witness there is significant testimony to the work of the Spirit in the life of the church as it ventures out into the world.

### The Affirmation of Scripture's Authoritative Witness to the Things of God

I like what Marcus Borg said about taking the Bible "seriously, but not literally." Perhaps a better way of putting it might be: "I take the Bible seriously, but not *necessarily* literally." This latter perspective, which I once heard from a Disciples biblical scholar, suggests that the Bible includes historical elements as well as metaphor. My point is that when Scripture is humbly and carefully interpreted and applied, making use of the resources of tradition, experience, and reason, it can serve as the norm in matters of faith and practice. It is this witness to God's work that guides our Christian faith and practice. Since we lack creeds, the Scriptures themselves become our normative creed. Michael Kinnamon and Jan Linn put it this way: "The conscious reaffirmation of the primacy of Scripture in Disciples life will necessarily also affirm our heritage as good thinkers who use our minds to understand the Bible."[8]

### The Affirmation That the Church Is the "Community of Faithful Worship, Witness, and Service in the World"

The blueprint model of restorationism puts limits on the way in which the church structures itself, as well as how the church worships. The Restoration Principle, on the other hand, invites us to engage the apostolic legacy that is present in the New Testament witness, which introduces us to a variety of structures and worship

---

7. Daugherty, "Under the Influence," 122–23.

8. Kinnamon and Linn, *Disciples*, 32–33.

styles. Therefore, it would seem appropriate for structures and styles of worship and governance to reflect changing times and places. The one thing that will remain constant is that the church is a community of the faithful who worship, witness, and serve together. In other words, from its very inception the church has been God's missional people.

## Conclusion

The Restoration Principle goes awry when we think we've recovered the whole truth and nothing but the truth, which means that we have nothing left to learn. This principle has value when it spurs within us an ongoing and unending search for truth and a commitment to finding "the integrity of faith."[9] It has value as long as it points us forward into the future, even as it provides us with a solid foundation in the past. Peter spoke of a time of "universal restoration" (Acts 3:21), a time when we will experience refreshment in the "presence of the Lord" (Acts 3:19–20). When that day comes, the nations will stream toward the mountain of the Lord, so that they might be taught by God and walk in God's ways. Then there will be peace and unity among all creation. Then, and only then, will the restoration of all things be complete (Isa 2:2–4). That is a restoration principle that we can and should embrace.

---

9. Toulouse *Joined in Discipleship*, 68; Hughes, "Subversion," 54.

# 4

# Unity—the Disciples' Vocation

POLITICS CAN BE STRIDENT and divisive. Candidates and their supporters often speak in black and white terms, even demonizing the other side. They do this to appeal to their base or brand. What is true of politics is true of many other areas of life. Consider college football: you can't root for the Oregon State Beavers and the Oregon Ducks, Kansas and Kansas State, or Michigan and Michigan State.

While college rivalries are largely fun in nature, political rivalries can have unfortunate consequences. They often lead to a polarized nation and in extreme cases civil wars. Consider how America has found itself divided into red and blue states. In the modern political culture, gridlock has taken root and nothing gets done, even as trust is broken with the citizenry. The message is: either you're for us, or you're against us. There is no room for compromise or neutrality. Politicians are often afraid of working with members of the other party, lest they engender a primary challenge on their right or left flank. This kind of situation might lead some to wonder if Rodney King had the right idea after the LA riots in 1992. Watching the aftermath of the trial of the police officers who beat him, he asked: "Can't we all just get along?" Regarding our political state, isn't purple a better shade of color than red or blue?

The church of Jesus Christ is not immune from polarizing conflicts. The church may be the body of Christ, but it is composed of imperfect human beings. Whether the issue is brand loyalty, ideology, social policy, or even worship style, it is very easy for us to demonize those whose opinions differ from ours. This tendency undermines the gospel, which should be marked by love, reconciliation, and inclusion. When people see Christians fighting amongst themselves they are right to ask: "Why can't you all just get along?"

Two centuries ago, Thomas and Alexander Campbell, along with Barton Stone, began asking that very question of their Christian neighbors, and it has been driving conversations among Disciples ever since. At the beginning of the twentieth century Disciples pastor and ecumenist Peter Ainslie said that the "greatest scandal of civilization is that Christians have not learned how to behave toward each other."[1] I suspect that it was this same concern that led Edgar DeWitt Jones, while serving as the pastor of Central Woodward Christian Church in the 1920s and 1930s, to answer the call to leadership in the national ecumenical movement.[2] The mission of God is compromised when the people of God fail to embrace Jesus' command to love their neighbors as they love themselves.

## Christian Unity: The Disciples' Cause

When it comes to finding unity in the midst of our many differences, Paul suggests that we look to Jesus, of whom he wrote: "In him the fullness of God was pleased to dwell, and through him God was pleased to reconcile to himself all things, whether on earth or in heaven, by making peace through the blood of his cross" (Col 1:19–20). Although humans have a tendency to break things, God is at work in Jesus putting things back together. If the church is the body of Christ, then wouldn't God want us to participate in this work of healing and reconciliation?

Disciples general minister and president Sharon Watkins has regularly declared that Disciples have an opportunity to bring

1. Ainslie, *Scandal of Christianity*, 1.

2. Edgar Dewitt Jones served as president of the Federal Council of Churches from 1938 to 1939.

either fragmentation or wholeness into the world. The choice is ours. As for her, she is choosing wholeness. Speaking for Disciples, she writes:

> We strive to welcome all, blurring human-made bound-aries, expanding the neighborhood at Jesus' instruction. We yearn for an experience of wholeness: unity, recon-ciliation, peace, and justice.[3]

When we look at the church, it's clear that we are a wounded and alienated body. Perhaps the image that could help us come to grips with this reality is that of the "wounded healer." It is as wounded healers, who are reconciled by God to Godself through Christ, that we can become agents of healing and transformation in the world. Unfortunately, we often wallow in our woundedness and allow our wounds to fester and hinder our participation in God's work of reconciliation.

The founders of the movement recognized that the church was broken, and they tried to fix it. Thomas Campbell said that division in the body of Christ was a "horrible evil" that required a commitment to healing the divide.[4] Put more positively, Barton Stone insisted that unity was our "polar star." While Disciples aren't the only Christians who pursue unity, unity stands at the center of our identity. At the same time that the founders recognized the problem of a divided Christian community, which they believed centered on adherence to theological opinions being enforced as the test of fellowship, they tended to impose a uniform church pol-ity. What resulted over the course of the history of the movement was, as Dwight Stevenson wrote as part of the Panel of Scholars reports from the early 1960s, that "we didn't quarrel over big ques-tions but about secondary matters, while the primary concerns which have troubled the great councils of the church through the centuries dropped into neglect."[5]

---

3. Watkins, Whole, 46.

4. Campbell, *Declaration and Address*, 16.

5. Stevenson, "Faith versus Theology," 54.

Given that our mission statement declares we are a "movement of wholeness in a fragmented world," if we as Disciples are honest, we will confess that from the beginning of this movement of reform we have been imperfect agents of reconciliation. We have experienced brokenness and have added our own brands to the Protestant world. Despite these failures, Christian unity is in our blood. As Kenneth Teegarden, a former general minister of the Christian Church (Disciples of Christ), put it:

> The ideal of Christian unity is to Disciples of Christ what basketball is to Indiana, hospitality is to the South, and nonviolence is to Quakers. It is part of our identity. It is our "middle name." It is "the plea"—the distinctive cause that has been the Christian Church's reason for existing.[6]

If we lose this sense of witness, then perhaps we would be wise to follow Barton Stone's initial decision to bury the Springfield Presbytery and merge into the broader Christian community.

## Christian Disunity—the Christian Dilemma

The world has changed dramatically since those early frontier days. For one thing, denominational brand identity isn't what it used to be. It is rare to find people today who have been part of one denomination all their lives. When you find people who are lifers, their loyalties are more likely given to local congregations rather than to denominations. Besides, unity sounds too much like uniformity.

When it comes to church shopping, the statisticians tell us that we live in a religiously generic age. The experts tell us that about 25 percent of Christians have switched their allegiance at least once, 20 percent have switched twice, and 10 percent have switched three or more times. What's more, I may be the poster child of this postdenominational world! I was born, baptized, and confirmed as an Episcopalian, but starting in high school I embarked on a journey across the religious spectrum that took

6. Teegarden, *We Call Ourselves Disciples*, 36.

me from Pentecostalism to the Disciples, with stops among the Baptists, Presbyterians, Christian Churches, and Evangelical Covenanters. It's no wonder that I've gotten involved in ecumenical and interfaith groups. It's in my blood!

We may easily shift from one tradition to another, being more concerned about what's happening at a local level than at a national level, but there was a time not so long ago when things were different. A few generations back many Protestants feared the election of a Roman Catholic president. Now the Supreme Court has a Roman Catholic majority. Where once Protestants and Catholics were just as willing to kill each other as cooperate, today it's possible for my wife, a Protestant since birth and married to a Protestant pastor, to have taught in Catholic schools.

As amazing as these changes are, there are other changes that might be even more amazing. Not only do churches cooperate with each other, they're reaching across religious boundaries to learn, to work, and even pray together. The congregation I currently serve has intentionally chosen to offer sacred space for people of all faiths to gather for both educational events and common prayer. We planted a rainbow-colored peace pole with the call to peace printed in eight languages, including Hindi, Arabic, Greek, Hebrew, and Pottawatomi (a Native American language), as well as English, Spanish, and German. We remain an ecumenical people, but the circle of our conversation has expanded beyond the Christian community.

Despite this good news, there are walls that still need to be taken down. These walls may no longer be denominational ones, but they still exist. Today's barriers are often cultural, ideological, ethnic, economic, and political rather than theological. The fact that Disciples have given priority to becoming an "anti-racist/pro-reconciliation" church is a reminder that we have not yet reached the post-racial promised land. As with many denominations, sexuality and sexual orientation remain divisive topics. Of course, in a politically polarized world our political divisions have a way of creeping into the conversation as well. We speak of an open table, but how open is our table really? As we ask this question of unity and openness, is it appropriate for us to recognize the value of our diversity? As Sandhya Jha points out in a helpful history of the struggle that non-white Disciples have had to find unity and equality within the movement, it is important that we understand and acknowledge "why those distinctions between communities might have occurred, and to examine our stories as a relevant part of the whole story of the Disciples."[7]

## The Call to Unity

While barriers to unity continue to exist in the church, Paul reminds us that "because there is one bread, we who are many are one body for we all partake of the one bread" (1 Cor 10:17). Each October Christians celebrate World Communion Sunday, an observance that reminds us that the table of unity and inclusion remains, for many Christians, a table of division and exclusion. It is often a place where only the initiated may enter. But is this truly reflective of Jesus' table fellowship? On the night of his betrayal, just moments before his arrest, he prayed for the unity of his disciples, that they would be one even as he and the Father were one (John 17:20–26).

The unity that Jesus prayed for can take many different forms. It can occur locally, regionally, nationally, and internationally. It can involve ecumenical institutions like the National Council of Churches, the World Council of Churches, Churches Uniting in Christ, or Christian Churches Together. After all, each of these institutions has had strong Disciples participation. It can also take place at a more personal level when we gather together with other Christians to pray, to study, and serve. Yes, there are walls that divide us, but these walls are not from God. As it is written in Ephesians: "There is one body and one Spirit, just as you were called to the one hope of your calling, one Lord, one faith, one baptism, one God and Father of all, who is above all and through all and in all" (4:3–6). God calls on us to be united, even as Jesus and the Father

7. Jha, *Room at the Table*, 2.

are united (John 17:20–21). It is our calling as Disciples and as Christians. Indeed, it is our calling as human beings, created in the image of God.

## The Purpose of Unity

From the earliest days of the movement of which the Disciples are but one branch, we have tried to bear witness to the importance of Christian unity. But what is the purpose of this unity? If we shouldn't compete with other Christian brands for customers, why do we exist as a separate entity? It is a question that was raised by Barton Stone and his colleagues who dissolved the Springfield Presbytery: "We will, that this body die, be dissolved, and sink into union with the Body of Christ at large; for there is but one body, and one Spirit, even as we are called in one hope of our calling."[8] This act of dissolving into the body of Christ at large didn't last long, as Stone joined in the creation of another entity designed to connect local congregations for ministry. Nonetheless, the "Last Will and Testament" is an important reminder that our denominational brands do not have ultimate significance.

Although the founders struggled to find a way to achieve true Christian unity, they believed that disunity was not the will of God. While we haven't been able to escape our own forms of division, their founding vision remains with us. Despite our own failures, we have continued to join in ecumenical ventures. It is in the Disciples DNA to do so.

One of the premises of the theory of evolution is that specific traits are retained from one generation to the next because they are beneficial to the organism. That may explain the ongoing commitment to unity—it is beneficial to our existence as a Christian communion.

The founders understood that the success of Christian mission on the frontier was dependent on building bridges to other Christian communities, so they could better reach out to a largely

8. Marshall et al., "Last Will," line 8.

unchurched region. Missionaries in places like China and Africa also discovered this to be true. If you're going bear witness to God's love for the world, especially one that is broken and divided, one that is full of violence, hatred, anger, ignorance, and disease, then the messengers need to exhibit a degree of wholeness if they're going to offer a faithful witness. If we remain divided, the effectiveness of this work of God in the world will be diminished.

Although non-institutionalized forms of religion ("spiritual but not religious") are gaining in popularity, institutional religion has the advantage of preserving and passing on important spiritual traits, that is, traditions of the faith. Generic forms of Christianity have found it difficult to continue to exist for more than a generation or two. They either institutionalize or they die. Besides, in this consumer-driven age generic forms tend to be more focused on relevance and success than in pursuing reconciliation. This makes the Disciples commitment to the ecumenical principle even more important. In embracing it we can encourage one another to join with God in breaking down the dividing walls and building bridges where chasms have developed. Yes, we can join together as wounded healers in the work of binding up the wounds of our world, for our witness is to God's wholeness.

# 5

# Harbingers of the Realm of God

DURING MY HIGH SCHOOL days I was really into eschatology, which is what theologians call the study of last things. I encountered a particular form of eschatology during those years through reading books such as Hal Lindsey's *Late Great Planet Earth*. Through his guidance I came to believe that I was living in the last days—that biblical prophecy was being fulfilled before my very eyes as I watched the six o'clock news. The message I read in those books was reinforced by the Christian music I was imbibing.

I remember listening with rapt attention as Barry McGuire transformed his 1960s-era anti-war protest song "Eve of Destruction" into an apocalyptic message of divine judgment, while Larry Norman offered a word of warning in "I Wish We'd All Been Ready." Along with reading expositions of apocalyptic theology accompanied by equally apocalyptic Christian rock music, we took time out at church for rapture practice—which involved jumping off chairs in the sanctuary. After all, my friends and I were convinced that Armageddon was close at hand. By our calculations taken from our reading of Hal Lindsey, the end should come sometime around 1988. A close look at the calendar demonstrates that our calculations were a bit off the mark. Apocalyptic imagery remains prominent in some Christian circles, with the *Left Behind* series becoming a staple on the *New York Times* Best Seller list. As a result, many both inside and outside Christianity believe that this is the normative Christian perspective.

While popular, this apocalyptic form of eschatology has never been the normative Christian perspective. It is in fact a rather recent development, at least in its current version. While the word "eschatology" sounds strange and exotic and isn't a word we likely use in normal conversation, it is an important topic of Christian conversation because it calls our attention to God's future. Therefore, even if we don't know the meaning of the word, we have most assuredly engaged in eschatological thinking.

Disciples have tended to shy away from apocalyptic forms of theology. Few Disciples churches host prophesy conferences or have rapture practices. Nevertheless, I believe Disciples have an "eschatological principle." While Alexander Campbell probably wouldn't qualify as an "end times" preacher, he did publish a journal that carried the title *The Millennial Harbinger*. How much more eschatological can you get than that?

## The Future and the Purpose of History

The title of his journal is a reflection of Campbell's belief in God's providence. He believed that God was at work in the world and that the events of today influenced the events of tomorrow. Like Martin Luther and John Wesley, Campbell had a Damascus Road experience. His first attempt at crossing the Atlantic from Scotland ended with a shipwreck, which delayed his move to America by a year. During that last year spent in Scotland, Campbell studied at the University of Glasgow and met some of the leading reformers of the day. As he waited for his opportunity to immigrate to America, he felt himself hearing God's call to join in the effort to reform the church and seek unity among all Christians. What happened in Glasgow that year significantly influenced the ministry he would have in America. As Campbell looked back at that shipwreck, he saw God's providential hand at work.

Believing that we should take seriously the events of the day because we don't know how they will influence tomorrow, Campbell began to perceive God's hand at work in his life. We might do the same. When I look back at my own life, I can find what might appear to be random events that, taken together, seem to have helped prepare me for my current ministry. It's not a matter of fate or determinism, but of a recognition that God seems to be leading me in a particular direction. Of course, we have to respond to the call. We play a significant role in creating our future, but the idea of providence suggests that God is actively engaged in this process with us.

## God's Stake in Human History

Alexander Campbell was confident that God "had a stake in human history."[1] Influenced by both his Reformed heritage and the Enlightenment vision of progress, Campbell and his reforming colleagues were not deists. Rather than believing that God set the universe in motion and then stepped out of the picture, they believed in a God who was present and active in the world.

Disciples have long valued the message of the book of Acts, a narrative that tells the story of God's activity in the world through the church that was born on Pentecost. As the book of Acts opens, Jesus stands before his gathered disciples. He tells them that while he was going to depart from them, he would not abandon them. When he was no longer physically present with them, God would send the Holy Spirit to be with them, empowering their witness as they went out into the world (Acts 1:6–8).

One could read the book of Acts as a meditation on God's unfolding work of grace in the world. If you read through to the end, you will discover that the book lacks a conclusion, much like the Gospel of Mark. When we get to the chapter 28 Paul is in Rome awaiting a trial that never seems to come. We are left wondering what became of him. By laying out the story in this way, Luke invites us into the continuing story of God's work in this world. The Christian community that emerges out of this early work of God's Spirit finds its roots in this story, making our story a continuation of Luke's story. If we understand our story as the continuation of

1. Toulouse, *Joined in Discipleship*, 127.

that commission in Acts 1:8 to go into the world and be Christ's witnesses, then we have an eschatological promise that guides us in our work today. The promise is this: God is not absent from our lives; instead, God is standing out in front of us, leading us and beckoning us into a future full of hope.

There are pessimistic eschatologies and optimistic ones. Some are fantasy and others are realistic. Some are focused on wars in heaven and on earth, but from the very beginning Disciples eschatology has been both hopeful and realistic. Disciples' eschatological musings have focused on the establishment of the realm of God here on earth, even as it is being established in heaven. This is, after all, the focus of the prayer most Disciples pray at least once a week in church.

Thinking eschatologically, we hear a message focused on God's work of reconciliation and healing of a broken world. It also lifts up the role we can play in God's work in the world. Ultimately, it is an invitation to love our neighbors even as we love ourselves. As Paul said, "In Christ, God was reconciling the world to himself" (2 Cor 5:19–20).

## The History of Salvation and the Future

We can deepen our eschatological vision by looking at history as the realm where God has engaged in the work of salvation. The biblical story itself offers a history of salvation. As Disciples biblical scholar Eugene Boring suggests, we might best understand the Bible as a five-act play: Creation, Covenant, Christ, Church, and Consummation.[2] History has a beginning and an end. It happened in the past, is happening in the present, and it will happen in the future. Standing at the very center of this salvation history is the promise that God will be with us every step of the way as we journey into the future. Our eschatological hope is that no matter how things look at this moment in time, God is reigning over all. Therefore, we need not live in fear.

2. Boring, *Disciples and the Bible*, 441–46.

The book of Revelation speaks to our questions of God's purpose and presence in difficult times. It might seem exotic and difficult to understand, but its basic point is quite simple: Even though things may look bad right now, hang tight because God will work things out. Rome might seem to be in control, but its leash is short. This bad news you've been hearing is not the last word. The messenger of God tells John, "Do not seal up the words of the prophecy of this book, for the time is near." Keep the book open because God is at work. Yes, both evil and good are present, but in time the good will prevail. So, again, just be patient!

We see this same eschatological message present in the parable of the mustard seed (Mark 4:30–32). According to the Gospel accounts, Jesus tells us that just like a mustard seed the reign of God starts small, but given time, it will grow just like the mustard seed, which is among the smallest of seeds but in time becomes a great bush. You might not see it just yet, but God is already reigning. Yes, the realm of God is in our midst. The old order may still be hanging on, kind of like a lame duck politician, but the signs of change are all around us. If we look hard enough, we'll see signs that God is at work. And if we listen closely, we'll hear God calling on us to join in this work of salvation.

## The Christian Eschatological Purpose—Salvation

Tony Dunnavant once wrote that Disciples have always been a "movement that understood itself in eschatological terms as one of God's instruments for the evangelization of the world."[3] It is our calling to be a harbinger of God's good news of healing and wholeness in this world. Our eschatological message isn't focused on promises of death and destruction for neighbors God chooses to leave behind. Instead, it is a word of hope and reconciliation.[4]

3. Dunnavant, "Evangelization and Eschatology," 51.

4. Cornwall, "Ministry of Reconciliation," 1–28. Although my own views have evolved since this was published, it speaks to the way in which Disciples understand mission and salvation.

In the closing verses of the book of Revelation, we hear a word of blessing along with an invitation. We hear the risen and triumphant Lord Jesus proclaiming to all who will listen: "Come . . . let everyone who wishes take the water of life as a gift" (Rev 22:17). This message, which John puts on the lips of Jesus, is also our message. Indeed, it is our good news.

There may be financial crises and seemingly unending wars, while poverty and disease appear to be ever present, but does this bad news have the last word? The answer is: Although the days ahead might get rough and be unsettling, God's reign will continue to spread. Not only that, but we get to participate in this work of reconciliation and healing.

The church's eschatological message is truly one of reconciliation, for God is at work in Christ reconciling the world to Godself (2 Cor 5:17). There is no better sign of this work of reconciliation than the Lord's Table, around which Disciples gather each Sunday, joining with brothers and sisters around the globe, celebrating the continual outpouring of God's love and grace.

The Lord's Table is one of two important markers of God's reign. The other is baptism. As Mark Toulouse puts it, "these two central sacraments of the church collapse God's time into our time and bring Christians to a firsthand encounter with God's grace in the here and now."[5] Baptism gives entrance into the kingdom, while the Lord's Supper anticipates the messianic banquet, when the hungry and the thirsty will be satisfied. When we share in them, we declare that God will reign over all.

If this is our eschatological calling, then perhaps our prayer as Disciples should be the one that John prays in closing his book: "Come Lord Jesus!" (Rev 22:20).

5. Toulouse, *Joined in Discipleship*, 128.

# 6

# The Sacred Ordinances

"A PICTURE IS WORTH a thousand words." There is much truth in this well-worn adage. If you look at a picture of two smiling young people facing each other and holding each other's hands as they stand before an altar, there is a good chance you know what is transpiring. You don't need words to explain the meaning of the picture, because the picture itself tells the story.

If you enter a church—and have some understanding of the Christian faith—and you see the Lord's Table set with a chalice and a loaf of bread, you will likely know what will occur in the near future. These ancient symbols of bread and cup bring to mind an ancient story about God's love for humanity, a love that was most fully expressed on a cross. Words may be shared, but the symbols themselves carry the story. What is true of the picture of the table is also true of a picture of a baptistery filled with water. It calls to mind a sacred covenant made by God with the recipients of baptism. Each symbol—table and baptistery—reminds us that while we are flawed human beings, we are recipients of divine grace. We know this to be true, because these symbols continue to speak to us, from one generation to the next.

## Why the Sacraments?

We call what happens at the table and baptistery "sacraments," and a sacrament is by common definition an "outward and visible sign of an inward and invisible work of grace." The word comes from the Latin, and it once referred to a sign of loyalty given to a military or political leader. In time the word took on a deeper religious meaning. It continued to convey a sense of loyalty, but in this case the object of loyalty was God. In Christian understanding, the external act became the sign of God's gracious work of transformation, which occurs internally. Over the years Christians have differed as to which sacred signs most explicitly carry this witness. Disciples have followed the Protestant practice and claim only two sacraments: baptism and the Lord's Supper. Although it's possible to expand the number, these two stand out.

Although it has become commonplace among Disciples to designate these signs as "sacraments," Disciples haven't always been comfortable with this term. Alexander Campbell didn't think the term was biblical enough. Ironically, he chose an equally non-biblical word—"ordinance"—to describe these two signs of divine grace. While Campbell did not use the word "sacrament," he did believe that Jesus had ordained these two actions of the church to be signs of God's grace. By whatever name these signs are called, they are understood to be divinely sanctioned. British Disciples theologian William Robinson wrote many years ago of the centrality of the Lord's Supper to the life of the church:

> Without elaborate ritual, then, and without vestments, Churches of Christ have found very satisfying, this worship centering in the Lord's Supper, conducted with dignity, simplicity, and quiet reverence, witnessing to the bond of fellowship which unites the members of the "beloved community" to one another and to their Divine Head, and which joins the Church on earth to the Church in heaven. Here in the Lord's Supper they have found a sure, yet silent witness to the Presence of the Lord, when in the fellowship company they have experienced the communion of the Body and Blood of Christ.[1]

As we will see in exploring both of these sacraments, the ritual might be simple but the meaning is both reformed and catholic.

1. Robinson, *What Churches of Christ Stand For*, 87.

## Baptism as a Means of Grace

It is Disciples practice to baptize by immersion following a confession of faith. Disciples have been doing this ever since Alexander Campbell decided not to baptize his infant daughter. Instead of following Presbyterian practice, he asked a Baptist preacher to baptize him, along with his father and their families. Born and raised Presbyterian, Campbell had been baptized as an infant, but after reading the New Testament he decided that believer's baptism by immersion was the clearest practice of the early church. He also decided that it should be the practice of modern churches as well.

The key to his new understanding of baptism can be found in his interpretation of Acts 2:38. Committed to restoring as much as possible the practices of the early Christians, Campbell found a pattern in Acts 2 that made sense to him. He determined that this was God's means of incorporating persons into the body of Christ, and that we should follow suit. When interpreting this decision, it is important to understand Campbell's context. In his own community and other faith communities, church membership was often limited to those who could narrate a conversion experience. Campbell came to believe that relying on religious experience led to uncertainty about one's status before God. It could also lead to false narratives of conversion. Being committed to a reasonable faith, his new reading of Acts 2:38 seemed to resolve these concerns.

Acts 2:38 recounts Peter's answer to a question posed to him after his Pentecost sermon. The crowd began asking him what they needed to do to be saved. Peter answered: "Repent, and be baptized every one of you in the name of Jesus Christ so that your sins may be forgiven; and you will receive the gift of the Holy Spirit." Campbell believed that if a baptism was done in good faith, God would honor this act of faith. One who had been baptized (by immersion) would have assurance of being a member of Christ's church and God's realm. Walter Scott, the lead evangelist among the founders, turned this passage into an evangelistic formula, which he called the "Five Finger Exercise." Scott would teach this exercise to children prior to his evangelistic meetings as a preview to his message. The message he would give focused on his understanding of the way of salvation: Belief, Repentance, Baptism, Forgiveness, and the Gift of the Holy Spirit. It was simple and effective, and it put baptism in context.

It is important to understand what stood behind Campbell's decision to move to this form of baptism. He believed that if we faithfully follow Christ's instructions, then God will be faithful to the promises attached to them. Therefore, if we truly repent of sins and receive baptism, then God will forgive our sins. It's not that the waters of baptism have magical powers. Rather, God is deemed faithful. This belief provided Campbell with the comfort and assurance that he was seeking. No longer was he dependent on a process that looked to religious experiences or feelings, which can be fickle, as confirmation that he was a member of God's family. The assurance of forgiveness that came with baptism was then accompanied by empowerment from the Holy Spirit who was given to the recipient in baptism.

Beyond this witness in Acts, we find other passages that deepen the meaning of the sacrament of baptism. Paul speaks of baptism being the event where we symbolically share in Jesus' death, burial, and resurrection. This is the place where we symbolically die to the old life while being buried with Christ in the waters of baptism. When we emerge from the water, we become a new person in Christ (Rom 6:1–11). In the Gospel of John it is said that one is to be "born again" or "born from above," and this is linked to being baptized in water and in the Spirit (John 3:1–10).

Beyond the soteriological elements of this baptismal theology, Disciples have understood baptism to be the place where Christians are ordained to the priesthood of all believers. Keith Watkins wrote that "no theological bar exists to any baptized believers who are designated by their congregation to baptize, administer the Lord's Supper, preach, teach or any of the other functions usually considered the prerogative of the ordained ministry of other traditions. Any other ordination to Christian ministry is secondary to Christian baptism."[2]

Baptism can be a life-changing experience because it so powerfully symbolizes the transformation that occurs within us when we choose to follow Jesus. It is true that we may stray from our commitments, but the memory of that event reminds us that God never strays from us. In this there is great joy!

Although Disciples practice believer's baptism (by immersion), ecumenical conversations led to the recognition that if Christians coming into a Disciples church from another Christian community had been baptized as infants or by a form other than immersion, then it would be inappropriate to require them to be rebaptized. This recognition led to the practice of open membership, wherein persons baptized in another tradition would be admitted to full membership without being immersed, in recognition that one should not presume to restrict God's work in the lives of Christians whose baptismal experience differs from that of the Disciples. While for many decades Disciples required rebaptism, deeming the baptism of non-immersed Christians to be deficient, the turn to open membership had roots in the practice of the churches that were related to the ministry of Barton Stone.[3]

## The Lord's Supper as Sacrament

The Lord's Supper is a sacrament known by a number of other names, including Holy Communion and the Eucharist. Due to the Disciples practice of weekly Communion, it stands at the center of our worship. As with baptism, Disciples find this sacrament to be present in Acts 2, where we find the early Christians gathering for worship and sharing in the breaking of the bread, along with listening to the teaching ministry of the apostles, sharing in community (fellowship), and gathering in corporate prayer (Acts 2:42).[4]

2. Watkins, *Baptism*, 20.

3. Toulouse, *Joined in Discipleship*, 140.

4. Cornwall, *Eucharist*.

Disciples have tried to follow this pattern by coming to the Lord's Table each Sunday. This practice is somewhat unique in Protestant circles, which is why a chalice was chosen as the Disciples' denominational symbol. It reminds us that the Table, more than anything else, defines us as a people. This is seen in the identity statement developed after the calling of Sharon Watkins to be general minster and president of the Christian Church (Disciples of Christ) in 2005: *"We are Disciples of Christ, a movement for wholeness in a fragmented world. As part of the one body of Christ, we welcome all to the Lord's Table as God has welcomed us."* As to the meaning of this statement, Watkins writes:

> The frequent television caricatures of Christianity are about dividing lines and stating who's in and who's out. The spiritual heart of my denomination, however, is a table where all are welcome because a loving God first welcomed us. It is a family table and much more. Food of symbolic nature is shared, but more important is the timeless, boundless embrace of the table's host, who is Jesus.[5]

In practice, not all congregations are as open with the table as are others, but in principle most Disciple congregations embrace an open table. Given that Disciples embrace the principle of freedom, one will find a variety of approaches and understandings present in Disciples congregations. Having said this, one should expect to find some common elements among these churches.

One of the most common beliefs about the Lord's Supper is that when we gather at the table we do so to *remember* Jesus' death on the cross. Following Jesus' own instructions as found in the New Testament, we break bread and drink of the cup in remembrance of Jesus (1 Cor 11:23–26). In remembering Jesus this way we are reminded that Jesus broke bread not only with his disciples, but also with sinners and tax collectors. Indeed, a close reading of the Gospels suggests that Jesus was quite indiscriminate about whom he invited to his table. The Table serves as a place to remember the life and teachings of Jesus, along with his death and resurrection.

5. Watkins, *Whole*, 20.

While Disciples Communion services often take on a memorialist demeanor, with a sober reverence marking the service, many congregations also emphasize Christ's continuing spiritual presence with the church at the Table. Jesus may not be present in the flesh with the gathered community, but spiritually he is present. Although Disciples do not believe that pronouncing the words of institution turn bread and juice into body and blood, in repeating the words shared by Jesus—"This is my body"; "This is my blood"—we are called upon to recognize the presence of the risen Christ in our midst. Belva Brown Jordan and Stephanie Paulsell perceptively capture the importance of this insight: "We find there the generous presence of Jesus, who saw and met the hunger of the crowds who gathered around him and who knows what we also need to be fed in order to follow him into the places he would have us go."[6] Just as we are called to remember his earthly life and death, we're also called to anticipate a final messianic banquet, which John the Revelator calls the "marriage supper of the Lamb" (Rev 19:9).

As Disciples place a special emphasis on the call the Christian unity, it should be expected that Communion is understood to be a sign of unity. In this regard, Paul wrote to the Corinthian church that because there is one bread and one cup, there is also one body of Christ (1 Cor 10:17). Thomas Campbell embarked on a new venture, pursuing Christian unity on the American frontier after recognizing the unfortunate message that a closed table sent to the broader community.[7]

We have a tendency to approach this meal with great sobriety, and for good reason. It is a sacred meal and it is observed as a remembrance of a life given for others. As we gather at the Table, we remember Jesus' sufferings on the cross, and surely that is sobering. But this is not a funeral service. We remember his death in the Supper, but we live in the shadow of the resurrection. Therefore, we should come to the Table with a sense of joy and celebration. Death isn't the final word, so as we come to the Table we can sing:

6. Jordan and Paulsell, "Lord's Supper," 157.

7. Cummins, *Disciples*, 42–43.

"I come with Joy, a child of God, forgiven, loved and free, the life of Jesus to recall in love laid down for me." As we share in this meal, we become a "new community of love in Christ's communion bread."[8]

Alexander Campbell understood that the meal was a sacred moment, but he also recognized the need for joy at the table. With that in mind he wrote: "with sacred joy and blissful hope [we] hear the Savior say, 'This is my body broken—this my blood shed for you.'"[9] It is this joy, and this hope, that move us to embrace one another in love. Indeed, in this call to the Table we hear a call to love the world even as Christ loves the world.

Disciples are indeed a sacramental people who celebrate God's grace by sharing in the waters of baptism and in Christ's messianic feast. These are visible signs of God's realm, which is already present in our midst.

---

8. Wren, "I Come with Joy," 420.

9. Alexander Campbell, *Restoration of the Ancient Order*, #6.

# 7

# Ministry without Hierarchy

THE DISCIPLES ARE NOT known for putting clergy on a pedestal. In fact, at times Disciples can be downright anti-clerical. There are both good and bad elements in such sentiments, but the roots of this ambivalence regarding clergy are to be found in the founders' commitment to the ministry of all believers. At her installation as general minister and president, Sharon Watkins acknowledged that Disciples don't do hierarchy very well. She's correct, as can be seen in Alexander Campbell's occasional condemnations of a "hireling ministry." A contributing factor in the division between the Disciples and the Churches of Christ (a division recognized formally in 1906) was the calling of resident preachers from outside the congregation.[1]

Despite this anti-clerical rhetoric, most Disciples churches have pastors who are both ordained and well-educated (the standard requirement for ordination is the completion of a Masters of Divinity degree or its equivalent). Most congregations look to these pastors to serve as their spiritual and administrative leaders. Over time Disciples came to recognize the value of having an educated and specialized form of ministry, even as they continued to affirm that every Christian has his or her own call to ministry. Therefore, ministry is much more than something that a pastor is

---

1. Williams et al., *Stone-Campbell Movement*, 79.

or does. Indeed, ministry is something that all Christians do, as ministry is a shared vocation.[2]

## An Evolving Theology of Ministry

Both the world and the church have changed greatly since the days of Alexander Campbell and Barton Stone. They practiced ministry in a rural and frontier context, where it was often difficult to obtain the services of an educated ministry (clergy). One of the reasons why the Disciples, Baptists, and Methodists thrived on the frontier was that they did not place a premium on specialized education or training, unlike Presbyterians, Congregationalists, and Episcopalians. Over the course of time the world changed, and with it came a belief among Disciples that they too would benefit from having an educated ministry. While the earliest educational institutions among disciples were colleges that sought to educate the whole community, in time seminaries began to emerge as congregations began to demand a specially trained ordained ministry.

Although churches have become accustomed to calling credentialed clergy to serve the congregation as pastor, declining membership and financial resources have forced many twenty-first-century Disciples congregations to consider what it would be like to live without a full-time ordained minister. Finding it difficult to afford the hiring of seminary-trained clergy, many congregations are returning to an earlier pattern of relying on lay elders for leadership, especially with regard to traditional sacramental functions. Be that as it may, if we reflect back on Campbell's view that every Christian is a minister, we can see the value he placed in making sure that all Christians received a thorough education in the Bible.

Taking up the work of his father, who served not only as a pastor but schoolteacher, Alexander Campbell established Bethany College to offer everyone in the church the possibility of receiving an education in the liberal arts and the Bible. This was important

2. Cornwall, *Unfettered Spirit*, 209–19; Cornwall, "Church and the Ministry of the Spirit," 463–76.

to Campbell because he believed that elders not only gave spiritual leadership to the congregation, but in most cases served as pastor of a congregation. Elders were charged with providing leadership, biblical teaching, and preaching. In most cases these leaders emerged from within the local congregation. This is one reason why the Disciples did so well on the frontier—congregations didn't have to wait around for a preacher to get started.

Things started to change after the Civil War. Disciples began to look at their neighbors, especially in the growing urban communities, and demanded educated ministers to serve their churches just like everybody else. When in 1862 Isaac Errett, then the pastor of a Detroit church, accepted the title of reverend, he received considerable opposition from other Disciples, making it clear that Disciples don't do hierarchy very well.[3]

As the frontier closed and people moved to towns and cities, the ministers of Disciples churches began to look like the ministers of the other Protestant churches. Errett may have been among the first to accept the nomenclature of the professional clergy, but before long many other Disciples ministers joined him in prefixing the title of reverend to their names. The desire for an educated clergy led to the founding of colleges and seminaries across the country, with the express purpose of training future preachers to fill the pulpits of Disciples churches. It was a natural change, but it did offer a challenge to traditional Disciples understandings of ministry.

As Disciples ministers pursued higher levels of education and took on a more professional sensibilities, their ranks were largely confined to men. The maleness of the clergy ranks has diminished over time, and women began to take on a greater variety of roles in the church during the twentieth century, including that of pulpit minister. While a majority of Disciples congregations continue to be served by male clergy, in 2005 the denomination called Sharon Watkins to be its general minister and president, making her the first woman to serve a mainline Protestant denomination in such capacity. Today the question before many regions and

3. Foster, "Isaac Errett," 302.

congregations concerns the recognition of the gifts and calling of those who happen to be lesbian, gay, bisexual, and transgender. Ordained ministry continues to be rooted in the ministry of the entire church, but how this ministry is understood and practiced continues to evolve.

Perhaps Alexander Campbell and Barton Stone would be a bit surprised with all the changes, but perhaps not. Visionaries in every age seem better able to adapt to the times, and in many ways these founders were visionaries. Still, the Disciples principle of ministry remains intact. Ministry is still something to which every Christian is ordained for in baptism. It does not matter whether one is clergy or laity.

## The Ministry of the People (Laos)

Baptism not only seals a person in the Christian faith and community, ushering a person into church membership, perhaps more importantly it serves to ordain that person for Christian ministry (Acts 2:38; 1 Cor 12:7). When it comes to ministry, baptism is the great equalizer. Whether clergy or laity, those who are baptized are ordained to ministry, and therefore all who are baptized are part of the *laos* or people of God.

All are gifted and called to be part of the *laos* ("laity"), but some are called to specialized forms of ministry that may require education, training, accountability, and professional standards. Nonetheless, all Christians are gifted and called to ministries of their own, whether that be caring for one's neighbors, engaging in intercessory prayer, participating in acts of compassion, sharing one's faith, or engaging in acts of justice. Every Christian is called to be an ambassador of reconciliation. Ministry is a shared vocation that emerges from within the congregation, which is the body of Christ, having as its head Jesus. For Disciples, Christ is the fountain of all ministerial authority, but that authority is mediated through the congregation.

Jesus doesn't just speak through preachers; Jesus speaks through the congregation. Although congregational government may not be the most efficient form of church governance, Disciples believe it is the one that allows Jesus to speak most freely.

## The Question of Ordination
## to Vocational Ministry

If ministry is a shared vocation to which all God's people are called, then what role do clergy play in the life of the church? While it is true that Disciples haven't always been comfortable with the idea of ordained clergy, by the end of the nineteenth century most Disciples churches had decided that it would behoove them to call to leadership in their churches persons (initially men) who had advanced training and recognized credentials. Where once they had looked inside the congregation for pastoral leadership, they increasingly looked beyond the congregation for such leaders. Once congregations began to look beyond the congregation for leadership, they needed to have confidence that the people they were calling were up to the task. In the beginning the focus was largely on education, but in time other questions emerged, such as clergy ethics and accountability. That concern led to the development of ministerial standards. Today Disciples regions are called on to implement standards of ministry developed by the General Commission on the Order of Ministry, and affirmed by vote of the General Assembly of the Christian Church (Disciples of Christ). In the course of time, matters of ordination and ministerial standing moved from congregations to regions, who carry out recommendations from the general Church.[4]

One study of ministry among the Disciples defined three fundamental tasks of pastoral ministry:

1. "Act in obedience to God's commandment of love in self-sacrifice on behalf of others and in a servant life in the world."

2. "Proclaim the gospel by word (teaching and preaching); by sacramental actions (Baptism and the Lord's Supper), and by deed (mission and service)."

4. Harrison, "Understanding of Ministry," 20–23.

3. "Oversee the life of the community in its worship, education, witness, mission, fellowship, and pastoral nurture."[5]

In one sense every Christian can fulfill these tasks, including that of oversight. But pastors serve the church in a representative way, by giving leadership to the church's ministries. Because Disciples do not have a sacramental understanding of ordination, those ordained to vocational ministry serve as representatives of the church, not representatives of Christ to the church. This is seen at the Lord's Table, where lay elders are deemed eligible to preside. Thus, while there is a recognized place for clergy in the life of Disciples congregations, they remain part of the *laos* of God.[6]

The Disciples understanding of ministry embraces the principle of freedom. Not only is there no hierarchy, but there are no predetermined doctrinal statements that must be affirmed. When I was ordained in 1985, I was asked to write a statement of faith at the beginning of the process and then write another at the end of the ordination process. The goal of this exercise was to discern whether there had been growth in my understanding of my faith. While Disciples do not have an extensive creedal statement to affirm, certain events in our history have led to the development of more precise standards of accountability.

Although not every Disciples pastor has earned a Master of Divinity degree, the General Commission on the Order of Ministry has determined that each commissioned or ordained minister should achieve a certain level of competency in sixteen areas, including theological and biblical studies, as well as preparation in areas of practical ministry.[7] One reason why Disciples have tightened standards of accountability over the years is the tragedy of Jim Jones and People's Temple. Although Jones was an ordained minister within the Disciples and People's Temple was a recognized Disciples congregation, when it became clear that Jones

5. "Word to the Church on Ministry," in Williams, *Ministry among Disciples*, 111.

6. Warner, "Meaning of Ordination," 70–71.

7. *Theological Foundations*, lines 413–19.

was acting in inappropriate ways the Disciples region in which he served had no power to hold him accountable.[8] In the intervening years, regions have taken steps to better oversee ministerial standing, which can be revoked if necessary. The basis of such actions, however, will not be doctrinal, but will be related to fitness for ministry.

What Disciples have learned over the years is that ministry is not an either/or proposition—either clergy or laity. Instead Disciples embraced a both/and position. There is room for both specialized forms of ministry that require special training and acknowledgment from the church, and the ministry of the whole people of God, including those called the "laity." The need for an educated ministry has been affirmed, whether or not that involves the earning of a particular degree, as well as the need for accountability of those called to commissioned and ordained ministry. In recognizing the value and validity of an ordained ministry, the church must wrestle with its anti-clerical heritage, lest congregations deem pastors to be simply employees hired to do their bidding, rather than persons called by God and gifted by the Spirit for this particular form of ministry. As a faith community that affirms the importance of freedom but seeks to live within a covenant relationship, the Disciples seek to keep in balance the calling of pastors with the ministry of the whole people of God, laity and clergy, male and female.

8. Cummins, *Disciples*, 241–42.

## Epilogue

# Disciples Living in
# Covenant Relationship

WE HAVE BEEN THINKING about basic foundational values and
principles that define the identity and practice of those who call
themselves Disciples of Christ. Disciples are marked by specific
principles: interpretation, restoration, ecumenical, eschatological,
sacramental, and ministerial. This is a community that is defined
by a commitment to liberty of thought and practice. Without a
hierarchy or a defining creedal statement, the question is: What
holds us together? What is the glue that binds us together as a
people? During the process of restructuring, which moved toward
being one church with three manifestations or expressions (local,
regional, general), Disciples leaders took hold of the idea of covenant. The question for us as Disciples concerns the nature of this
covenant.

Throughout the Bible we read about covenants. God makes
a covenant with Noah, with Abraham and Sarah, and with Israel
through Moses. Jeremiah speaks of a new covenant, one that will
be written on the heart rather than stone (Jer 31). Jesus describes a
covenant that was made in his blood—the Eucharist (Luke 22:20).
It is also the word that was chosen to describe the relationship of
the local, the regional, and the general manifestations of the Christian Church (Disciples of Christ).

In the Preamble to *The Design for the Christian Church
(Disciples of Christ)*, the document that defines and governs the

organizational structure of the Christian Church (Disciples of Christ), Disciples make this confession: "We rejoice in God, maker of heaven and earth, and in the covenant of love which binds us to God and one another."[1] *The Design* defines the relationship of local, regional, and general expressions of the denomination in this way:

> Within the universal Body of Christ, the Christian Church (Disciples of Christ) is identifiable by its testimony, tradition, name, institutions, and relationships. Across national boundaries, this church expresses itself in covenantal relationships in congregations, regions, and general ministries of the Christian Church (Disciples of Christ), bound by God's covenant of love. Each expression is characterized by its integrity, self-governance, authority, rights, and responsibilities, yet they relate to each other in a covenantal manner, to the end that all expressions will seek God's will and be faithful to God's mission. We are committed to mutual accountability. The Christian Church (Disciples of Christ) confesses Jesus Christ as Lord and constantly seeks in all of its actions to be obedient to his authority.[2]

Ronald Osborn, one of the leaders of the 1960s movement to restructure the way the Disciples live together, reflected on the nature of this covenant relationship that binds Disciples together:

> In religion, in marriage, and in the life of a nation, a covenant is a sacred bond sealed with an oath or vow of allegiance. In the community of Christians that pledge is called a sacrament. A Christian swears faithfulness to God. God promises faithfulness to the church. This two-way pledge is seen most clearly in the Christian covenant-sacraments of baptism and communion.[3]

Osborn speaks of the sacraments of baptism and the Lord's Supper as being signs of this covenant relationship, but what is required of the parties involved in this covenant relationship? Besides

1. *Design*, p. 1, lines 10–13.
2. Ibid., p. 1, line 41 to p. 2, line 7.
3. Osborn, *Faith We Affirm*, 59.

the sacramental signs, what are the practical signs of covenant relationship?

Disciples leaders in the 1960s chose the term "covenant" very purposely. They did this because prior to the restructure Disciples understood themselves to be an autonomous fellowship of churches and mission agencies. That is, the relationship between the various entities that marked the Disciples movement was voluntary. Congregations were self-governing. Agencies, including missionary agencies, were accountable to themselves, and only tangentially to the International Convention of the Christian Churches (Disciples of Christ). The same was true of state conventions as well.

Although Disciples began to use covenant language and changed the name of the denomination from Christian Churches (Disciples of Christ) to Christian Church (Disciples of Christ), signifying that we had moved from a collection of churches to seeing our extra-congregational expressions as church in the same way that congregations are considered church, the legacy of that pre-restructure view still pervades our churches. It is common for Disciples to hold strong views of congregational autonomy. We hear it in conversations among clergy, at regional events, in congregations, and at general assemblies. When the general assembly votes on an issue, such as whether to fully welcome LGBT Christians into our churches, it is made clear that this is only a word of advice to the churches. Therefore, it does not require anything of either regions or congregations.

The use of covenant language provides an important theological foundation to the denomination's identity, but how does this work out in practice? How might the three expressions of this one church express its unity of purpose as a covenant community? One important way in which congregations can demonstrate their commitment to the covenant relationship with the general and regional expressions of the church is through financial support through participation in the Disciples Mission Fund (DMF). It is through giving to DMF that Disciples support the ministries of the general church, including the Global Ministries, Homeland

Ministries, Higher Education and Leadership Ministries, and the Office of the General Minister and President, as well as Regions. The question that often comes up in conversations among Disciples—often offered up by clergy—concerns why local congregations should give to the denomination or support the region In other words, what's in it for us? When the conversation goes in this direction, giving to DMF is seen as payment for services rendered, not as a sign of covenantal commitment to the welfare of the broader church. However, regular giving through DMF, like regular giving to a congregation, stands as a strong sign of commitment to the covenant relationship. This is but one way in which the local congregation can give evidence of its commitment to the wider church/denomination.

In designing the restructured denomination, those engaged in the work sought to be true to the Disciple heritage of avoiding hierarchy, and therefore each manifestation or expression of the church is understood to be equal to the others. While Disciples have not made Trinitarian theology a defining element of its life together, one can see a parallel between the way the covenant relationship is formed and the way Christians have understood the relationship of the three persons of the Trinity. Each is different, and yet each is equal to the other.

In keeping with the commitment to unity, it should not be surprising that the relationship between the Disciples as a denomination and other denominations in the Christian world should be seen in covenant terms. In this regard, Ronald Osborn wrote:

> Bound to God and to all God's people in sacred covenant, we can never think of the Christian community as limited to our own particular denomination. By our baptism we are united with the one body; at the table of the Lord we reaffirm our oneness with all who own the Lordship of Christ.[4]

Although Disciples have embraced this covenant language, there remains a strong tendency to speak of the relationship

4. Ibid., 66.

between congregations and regions and the general church as being one of "affiliation" rather than "covenant." In a legal sense, there may not be much of a difference, but theologically there is a significant difference of understanding. Affiliation—at least to me—speaks of a convenient relationship that lasts as long as the other party serves my needs. Taken theologically, a covenant is not something easily broken. It is a two-way commitment to the welfare of the other. Thus, as members of a local congregation, we stand in covenant relationship with God, who then binds us together with one another, both inside and the congregation (John 17:20–26). As a Disciple, I understand that I live within a covenant relationship that involves congregation, region, general church, and the broader ecumenical community. For are we not all one in Christ? (Gal 3:28).

Yes, the Disciples are a people who value freedom. There is no hierarchy or belief system that is imposed on individuals, congregations, regions, or general expressions. There is instead a commitment to live together as one people, sharing certain principles and traditions that give a sense of rootedness and guidance to these relationships. While there is indeed a great deal of autonomy inherent in these relationships, it is not a complete or absolute autonomy. For the Disciples to truly be a communion, this covenant relationship must be owned and lived in practical ways. Lip service to covenant undermines the community's life together. If the covenant we claim to affirm is lived out in practice, then the freedom that Disciples prize takes on a whole new dimension. When we live out the covenant, the church as a whole will become that communion whose time really has come. If this communion called the Christian Church (Disciples of Christ) truly embraces the covenant we claim to affirm, then we as a denomination will be in a position to be a blessing to the world we inhabit.

# Bibliography

Ainslie, Peter. *The Scandal of Christianity*. New York: Willett, Clark, & Colby, 1929.

Allen, Ronald J. "The Church as a Community of Conversation." In *Under the Oak Tree: The Church as Community of Conversation in a Conflicted and Pluralistic World*, edited by Ronald J. Allen et al., 204–16. Eugene, OR: Cascade, 2013. Kindle edition.

Boring, M. Eugene. *The Disciples and the Bible: A History of Disciples Biblical Interpretation in North America*. St. Louis: Chalice, 1997.

Boring, M. Eugene, and Fred B. Craddock. *The People's New Testament Commentary*. Louisville: Westminster John Knox, 2009.

Campbell, Alexander. *Restoration of the Ancient Order*, number 6. Online: http://godsbreath.net/2012/10/11/restoration-of-the-ancient-order-6.

Campbell, Thomas. *Declaration and Address*. In *Pioneer Sermons and Addresses*, edited by F. L. Rowe, 14–104. Cincinnati, 1908. Reprint, Joplin, MO: College Press, n.d.

Cornwall, Robert D. *The Authority of the Bible in a Postmodern Age: Some Help from Karl Barth*. Gonzalez, FL: Energion, 2014.

———. "The Church and the Ministry of the Spirit." *Encounter* 59 (1998) 463–76.

———. *The Eucharist: Encounters with Jesus at the Table*. Gonzalez, FL: Energion Publications, 2014.

———. "The Ministry of Reconciliation: Toward a Balanced Understanding of the Global Mission of the Christian Church (Disciples of Christ)." *Lexington Theological Quarterly* 30 (1995) 1–28.

———. *Unfettered Spirit: Spiritual Gifts for the New Great Awakening*. Gonzalez, FL: Energion, 2013.

Cummins, D. Duane. *The Disciples: A Struggle for Reformation*. St. Louis: Chalice, 2009.

Daugherty, Dyron. "Under the Influence: Pneumatology in Global, Historical Perspective." In *Chalice Introduction to Disciples Theology*, edited by Peter Goodwin Heltzel, 116–23. St. Louis: Chalice, 2008.

*The Design for the Christian Church (Disciples of Christ).* 2013. Online: http://disciples.org/Portals/0/PDF/TheDesign.pdf.

Dunnavant, Anthony. "Evangelization and Eschatology: Lost Link in the Disciples Tradition?" *Lexington Theological Quarterly* 28 (1993) 43–54.

Dunnavant, Anthony, et al. *Founding Vocation & Future Vision: The Self-Understanding of the Disciples of Christ and the Churches of Christ.* St. Louis: Chalice, 1999.

Epperly, Bruce G. *Process Theology: A Guide for the Perplexed.* New York: T. & T. Clark, 2011.

Foster, Douglas A. "Isaac Errett." In *The Encyclopedia of the Stone-Campbell Movement*, edited by Douglas A. Foster et al., 301–33. Grand Rapids: Eerdmans, 2004.

Guarino, Thomas G. *Vincent of Lérins and the Development of Christian Doctrine.* Grand Rapids: Baker Academic, 2013.

Harrison, Richard L. "The Understanding of Ministry in the History of the Christian Church (Disciples of Christ)." *Lexington Theological Quarterly* 1 & 2 (2002) 7–26.

Hughes, Richard T. "The Subversion of Reforming Movements." In *Founding Vocation and Future Vision: The Self-understanding of the Disciples of Christ and the Churches of Christ*, by Anthony L. Dunnavant et al. St. Louis: Chalice, 1999.

Hughes, Richard T., and C. Leonard Allen. *Illusions of Innocence: Protestant Primitivism in America, 1630–1875.* Chicago: University of Chicago Press, 1988.

Jha, Sandjha. *Room at the Table: Struggle for Unity and Equality in Disciples History.* St. Louis: Chalice, 2009.

Jones, Edgar DeWitt. *A Man Stood Up to Preach.* St. Louis: Bethany, 1941.

Jordan, Belva Brown, and Stephanie A. Paulsell. "The Lord's Supper." In *Chalice Introduction to Disciples Theology*, edited by Peter Goodwin Heltzel, 152–59. St. Louis: Chalice, 2008.

Kinnamon, Michael, and Jan Linn. *Disciples: Reclaiming Our Identity, Reforming Our Practice.* St. Louis: Chalice, 2009.

Marshall, Robert, et al. "The Last Will and Testament of the Springfield Presbytery." Online: http://en.wikisource.org/wiki/Last_Will_and_Testament_of_The_Springfield_Presbytery.

Osborn, Ronald. *Experiment in Liberty.* St. Louis: Bethany, 1978.

———. *The Faith We Affirm: Basic Beliefs of Disciples of Christ.* St. Louis: Chalice, 1979,

Pelikan, Jaroslav. *The Vindication of Tradition.* New Haven, CT: Yale University Press, 1984.

Pinnock, Clark H. *Most Moved Mover: A Theology of God's Openness.* Grand Rapids: Baker Academic, 2001.

Robinson, William. *What Churches of Christ Stand For.* Birmingham, UK: Berean, 1946.

Stevenson, Dwight. "Faith versus Theology in the Thought of the Disciples Fathers." In *The Reformation of Tradition*, edited by Ronald E. Osborn, 33–60. The Panel of Scholars Reports 1. St. Louis: Bethany, 1963.

Stone, Barton W. "To the Church Scattered throughout America." In *Pioneer Sermons and Addresses: Restoration Reprint Library*, compiled by F.L. Rowe, 149–62. Cincinnati, 1908. Reprint, Joplin, MO: College Press, n.d.

Tabbernee, William. "Theology and Tradition." In *Chalice Introduction to Disciples Theology*, edited by Peter Goodwin Heltzel, 45–53. St. Louis: Chalice, 2008.

Teegarden, Kenneth. *We Call Ourselves Disciples.* St. Louis: Bethany, 1975.

*Theological Foundations and Policies and Criteria for the Ordering of Ministry of the Christian Church (Disciples of Christ).* 2014. Online: http://disciples. org/Portals/0/PDF/TFPCOM/TFPCOM-Final.pdf.

Toulouse, Mark G. *Joined in Discipleship: The Shaping of Contemporary Disciples Identity.* Rev. ed. St. Louis: Chalice, 1997.

Warner, Sharon. "The Meaning of Ordination in the Church." *Lexington Theological Quarterly* 1 & 2 (2002) 61–84.

Wilburn, Ralph G. "The Lordship of Jesus Christ over the Church." In *The Reconstruction of Theology*, edited by Ralph G. Wilburn, 170–90. The Panel of Scholars Reports 2. St. Louis: Bethany, 1963.

Watkins, Keith. *The American Church That Might Have Been: A History of the Consultation on Church Union.* Eugene, OR: Pickwick, 2014.

————. *Baptism and Belonging: A Resource for Christian Worship.* St. Louis: Chalice, 1991.

Watkins, Sharon. *Whole: A Call to Unity in Our Fragmented World.* St. Louis: Chalice, 2014.

Williams, D. Newell. *Ministry among Disciples: Past, Present, and Future.* The Nature of the Church 3. St. Louis: Christian Board of Publication, 1985.

Williams, D. Newell., et al., editors. *The Stone-Campbell Movement: A Global History.* St. Louis: Chalice, 2013.

Wren, Brian. "I Come with Joy." In *Chalice Hymnal*, 420. St. Louis: Chalice, 1995.